2-18-60

Seven Editors

by Harold Herd

THE MARCH OF JOURNALISM
THE MAKING OF MODERN JOURNALISM
THE NEWSPAPER OF TOMORROW
etc.

HAROLD HERD

Seven
Editors

———

GEORGE ALLEN & UNWIN LTD
RUSKIN HOUSE
MUSEUM STREET LONDON

*Printed in Great Britain
in 10 point Caledonia type
by East Midland Allied Press, Ltd
Kettering, Peterborough and elsewhere*

INTRODUCTION

In the writing of *The March of Journalism*,[1] the story of the British Press during three centuries, the extensive research which had to be undertaken led me into many fascinating bypaths and brought to light some interesting and little-known personalities; but these could be only briefly treated in a work that compresses 330 years of journalistic history into a single volume.

There was, for example, what I now call The Strange Case of the Murdered Editor: this would obviously require further investigation at leisure. When after long hours of research I found that I had uncovered a 120-years-old news story that had gone unreported at the time, when I considered the extraordinary mystery —perhaps as insoluble as the historic riddle of who killed Sir Edmund Berry Godfrey—surrounding the death of one of the foremost journalists of his day, the idea of the present volume was born. It is, in effect, a series of footnotes to the history of journalism.

The subjects chosen have only two points in common—they were all editors and they were all (or nearly all) remarkable men. Six of them were British and one American: I have included James Gordon Bennett because, though the story of his exuberant career is familiar to all American journalists, it is only sketchily known on this side of the Atlantic.

With the one exception of William Hone, hardly anything has been written in the present century about the six British editors portrayed here; but, as may be seen, this is not for lack of rich and picturesque material.

H. H.

[1] George Allen and Unwin, 1952.

CONTENTS

The Decline and Fall
of Eustace Budgell

*

THE trial by newspaper and pamphlet of Eustace Budgell is one of the most remarkable episodes in the history of journalism, yet apart from professional students of the Grub Street period few people are acquainted with it or with the fact that he produced one of the earliest digest magazines.

The idea of a digest of current publications, which has been so successfully exploited in modern times by the *Reader's Digest* and numerous other pocket magazines in many languages, goes back to the beginnings of periodical journalism. There were few periodicals published in this country at the time that Edward Cave, from his printing office at St. John's Gate, Clerkenwell, added to their number a monthly that appears to have been the true begetter of the digest as well as the first publication to call itself a magazine—the *Gentleman's Magazine*, founded in 1731.[1]

This notion of a journal that would give a selection of essays and intelligence from newspapers and magazines

[1] 'This Consideration has induced several Gentlemen to promote a Monthly Collection to treasure up, as in a Magazine, the most remarkable Pieces on the Subjects abovemention'd' (*Gentleman's Magazine*). Cave's previous experience included the publishing of a newspaper at Norwich and, while he was working in the Post Office in London, the supplying of newsletters to a number of provincial journals, so that he may be said to be the pioneer also of syndication and of the London letter feature. 'His mental faculties were slow. He saw little at a time, but that little he saw with great exactness,' said the writer of the three-page biography published in his magazine when he died in 1754.

had been in Cave's mind for years but he could not interest printers or booksellers in the idea: when he eventually issued it himself the public reception was so favourable (early numbers had to be reprinted several times) that imitators soon came into the field. Cave has another important claim to a niche in the history of British journalism, since he stubbornly persisted for years in reporting Parliamentary debates, despite the displeasure of the House of Commons; but that is a story that has often been told. The *Gentleman's Magazine* survived in substantially the same form for about a century and a half, long outliving all its imitators, including the *Magazine of Magazines* (1750), a title that anticipated by 140 years W. T. Stead's *Review of Reviews*.

Among those who were attracted by the possibilities of this new journalistic invention was Eustace Budgell, who was to become the target of Grub Street spite at its most venomous and to earn cruel immortality through one of Pope's most pointed couplets. The petty rivalries and the criss-cross of mean intrigues in Grub Street, of which we have glimpses in the *Dunciad* and various works of the period, form a shabby and confusing chapter in literary history that is difficult to study without impatience and disgust; but two or three figures emerge out of the murk of controversy with a distinctness that enables us even at this distance of time to get a reasonable grasp of why they so violently irritated their contemporaries.

The story of the decline and fall of Eustace Budgell, founder and editor of the *Bee*, can be traced clearly in the chronicles of his time. His beginnings were propitious and make the subsequent tragedy all the more poignant; vain and pompous and unscrupulous though he appears to posterity, it is impossible not to be moved by the tragedy of his downfall. The son of a doctor of divinity, he was born in 1686 and matriculated at Trinity College, Oxford, in 1705 and was afterwards called to the Bar. But he did not take up a legal career, family influence (a main ingredient of success in those days) taking him into public life as well as making an opening for him in literature under the best auspices. Addison, who was his cousin, took a liking to him, and while serving as Secretary to Lord Wharton, the Lord Lieutenant of Ireland, found a place for Budgell in his office. For several years Budgell shared Addison's lodgings, and it was no doubt through the latter's introduction that he contributed to the *Tatler* and the *Spectator*. He is credited with at least twenty-eight essays in the *Spectator*—and according to Dr. Johnson, speaking long after the event, Addison 'mended them so much that they were almost his own.' When the *Spectator* was revived on June 18, 1714, Budgell was a partner with Addison and looked after the routine side of the paper—now published thrice weekly instead of daily. Like many revivals it was only moderately successful, and Addison soon tired of the venture. His last contribution appeared on September 29 of the same year, and the thirty-five further issues published to complete the eighth volume were supervised by Budgell.[1] In 1714 Budgell published a translation of *The Moral Character of Theophrastus*. Three years earlier his father had died and left him an estate of £950 a year.

When Addison was again appointed Chief Secretary for Ireland on the accession of George I (1714) he made his cousin Under-Secretary. Budgell now began to play an important part in public life—but four years later the career of this fortunate young man was in ruins, and after that nothing ever seemed to go right again. He was made Chief Secretary of the Lords Justices and Deputy Clerk of the Council, and sat in the Irish Parliament as M.P. for Mullingar. In 1717, through the influence of Addison, he was appointed Accountant and Controller-General of the Revenue in Ireland, but in the following year, having

[1] *The Life of Joseph Addison*, by Peter Smithers (Oxford University Press, 1954).

quarrelled with the Secretary to the new Lord Lieutenant (Lord Bolton), he lost his places.

On his return to England he published a pamphlet
(*A Letter to the Lord—from Eustace Budgell, Esq., Ac-
comptant-General of Ireland, and late secretary to their
Excellencies the Lord Justices in that kingdom*) dealing
with the affair which was said to have caused embarrassment to Addison. A greater misfortune came when he
lost £20,000 (according to his own statement in *Liberty
and Property*) in the South Sea Bubble. In this book he
asserts that the Duke of Portland, who proposed to make
him his secretary when he became Governor of Jamaica,
was informed by the Secretary of State that he could
have any man in England for the post except Budgell.
Unsuccessful attempts to get into Parliament were said
to have cost him £5,000 of his own money and £1,000
given to him by the Duchess of Marlborough; various
law-suits added to his vexatious troubles, and he conceived the idea that a clergyman with whom he had
litigation over an estate (there is much confused stuff
about this dispute in *Liberty and Property*) had the
backing of Robert Walpole.

This was not his only delusion: he believed that he was
dogged by spies and declared that various attempts had
been made upon his life. Once he presented a petition to
George II demanding the punishment of Walpole. Several
pamphlets that he wrote dealt with his grievances and
his lawsuits. All the evidence suggests that his mind had
been affected by his many reverses.

The fifteen years after the collapse of his public career
are a melancholy record of decline. A few influential
people still had confidence in him: he found a useful
protector in an enemy of Walpole, the Earl of Orrery,
who made him his secretary. When the latter died in
1731 Budgell wrote *Memoirs of the Life and Character
of the late Earl of Orrery and the Family of the Boyles,*

which went into several editions over a period of years. He began to be known in Grub Street and became a contributor to Nicholas Amhurst's *Craftsman,* the leading political journal of the age. If he had died at this time his name would have survived only as a footnote to the history of the *Spectator,* but in 1733 he boldly started a magazine and was bitterly assailed by one of his competitors, and in the same year he was involved in a shady affair that delivered him into the hands of his numerous enemies in Grub Street and brought about the final disaster of his unhappy life.

The *Gentleman's Magazine* and its first imitator the *London Magazine* (which continued publication for nearly fifty years) were both monthlies. Budgell decided that there was an opening for a weekly on the same lines. The name he selected for his digest magazine was *The Bee: or, Universal Weekly Pamphlet,* 'Containing Something to hit Every Man's Taste and Principles.' The cover had a drawing of a beehive with bees flying towards it bringing scraps of paper typifying extracts from newspapers and books scattered on the ground. The first number, octavo size, contained 44 pages. The editorial programme was set forth with disarming candour:

'Our BEE will contain an Abridgment of every thing Material, and all the Essays worth reading in the Weekly Papers; with some Original Compositions, both in Prose and Verse. It is likewise to contain an Account of Foreign Affairs and Domestick Occurrences, in a much better Stile and Manner than any News Paper now extant. . .

'We must ingenuously confess, that our BEE's sucking out the Quintessence of every Publick Paper, rifling all its sweets, extracting its best Parts, and rejecting the rest, seems to carry such an Air of Piracy, and to give us so unfair a Superiority over all other Papers, that we should have made some scruple to have taken this Matter, if it had not been already put in Practice by several Persons before us: We dare assure those Gentlemen who write in any of the Publick Papers, that they will find themselves used, at least, with as much candour and Justice in the BEE, as they have hitherto been in any other Pamphlet.'

Budgell issued his weekly unstamped and raged at the authorities when they decided after some issues had appeared that it was a newspaper and therefore liable to threepence duty. He represented this ruling as an act of suppression—as an attack on the freedom of the Press. The magazine did not appear for three weeks. He changed the title to *The Bee: or, Universal Weekly Pamphlet Revived;* later the title became *The Bee Revived: or, the Universal Weekly Pamphlet.* For many issues, and almost to the last number (118 were published in all), the title page contained this note: 'This Pamphlet was suppressed, after Number X, by certain Persons, for certain Reasons, in such a Manner as was never heard of before in a Free Nation.' A preface to No. XIV, after a reference to the three weeks' interruption of publication, went on: 'Tho' we shall at present say nothing more of this Affair, we conceive it might not be amiss to give our Posterity some Account of it, should they ever happen to peruse the BEE; We shall therefore prefix to this Volume the following Letter wrote by a Gentleman who is one of our Society.' The letter, eight pages in length, was signed by Budgell. He told how he came to start the *Bee:* 'Having been stripped of an handsome Fortune, I was born to, by a Train of wicked Arts too long to trouble you with an Account of, and having some leasure Time, I resolved to employ those little natural Talents, which Heaven has given me, for the Diversion and Instruction of the Publick, and my own Advantage. . . I have the strongest Reasons to believe, that certain Persons will never forgive my having thrown myself in your Defence, during your late Struggle for your Liberties and Trade. I have reason to believe, that this is the true Cause of the Usages I endure at present.'

The *London Magazine* seized the chance to strike at its rival. It gloated over Budgell's discomfiture. In an article published in the issue for May, 1733, under the sensational title of 'The Downfall of the BEE,' the magazine was held up to scorn as a 'Weekly Hodge-Podge, consisting of a very dull Repetition of what was published the Week before, and an unjust Pyratical Insertion of the Properties of other People.' It was contended that the *London Magazine* was a very different thing, being compiled from newpapers several of which they owned themselves, whereas Mr. Budgell's *Bee* was 'nothing more than a direct Pyracy of what every Bookseller in Town printed, not having the least property in any Thing but his own Vanity and Assurance.' The *London Magazine*, a shameless example of imitation, should have been the last journal to adopt this self-righteous attitude. It had brazenly adopted every detail of the *Gentleman's Magazine* formula, the contents and the titles of the features being deliberately copied. Many years later the *Gentleman's Magazine*, in its obituary of Cave, mildly remarked that although the trade had not thought his idea worthy of a trial this was not because they were restrained by their virtue from executing another man's design, as many imitations of his magazine revealed when the design was seen to be gainful; and it attributed the success of the *London Magazine* to the backing of a powerful association of booksellers. Eustace Budgell, who could at least claim that the *Bee* was not designed to look like the *Gentleman's Magazine*, struck at his rival in its most vulnerable spot:

'The very Plan of their Magazine, if there is any Thing tolerable in it, is so far from being their own, that they stole even this, from Mr. Cave the Printer. . . It is certain, that Part of our BEE is an Extract from other papers:

yet we hope that Extract is made with some Judgment, and, perhaps, our Readers are much more obliged to Us than they imagine, for separating the grain from the Chaff, for their Use. . . We have hardly published a single BEE, in which there have not been several Original Compositions, either in Prose, or Verse, or in Both.'

Reporting progress in his preface to the third volume, Budgell wrote:

'Our BEE is already translated and published twice a Week at Hamburgh,[1] from whence he flies over all Germany; We have reason to believe, that he will soon be translated into French, in order to make his Appearance at Paris; and since we find he is so much taken notice of in Foreign-Parts, we shall do our best that he may be no disgrace to the Island of Great-Britain, his Native Country.'

The *Bee* continued publication for over two years, and in an introduction to the final volume Budgell explained that some gentlemen who had assisted him with the magazine had not cared to carry on without him and that as he required to employ his time for three or four months 'upon some other Things' he had decided to suspend publication but intended to resume it in the Winter.

But the *Bee* had run its course. Not one of its readers could have been unaware that the fortunes of Eustace Budgell had decisively set. Within its pages he had been defending not only his magazine but his personal honour. His enemies in Grub Street, led by Edmund Curll, the notorious bookseller, were in full cry. Curll was able to combine profit with vengeance on Budgell by his publication of the forged will of Dr. Matthew Tindal, the well-known deist, who had recently died at the age of 76. A

---

[1] Budgell's magazine was possibly the first digest to have a foreign edition.

second printing of this pamphlet was quickly called for.

Calmly reviewed over two centuries later, the known facts in the case appear to justify the verdict of his contemporaries that Budgell had forged the will to his own advantage and substituted it for the genuine one. The Rev. Nicholas Tindal, nephew of the theologian and the translator of Rapin (and later to acquire a considerable reputation as historical writer), had expected to be the sole heir; but when his uncle died on August 16, 1733, a will was produced dated only nine days earlier under which the main bequest was one of £2,000 to Eustace Budgell 'that his great Talents may serve his country' (a phrase that to careful students of his style must have had a suspiciously Budgellian ring). A further bequest provided that Budgell should have 'my Strong-Box, my Diamond Ring, and all my Manuscript Books, Papers and Writings, and I do hereby desire the said Eustace Budgell to print the second part of *Christianity as Old as the Creation* and also my others Works collected in a Volume.' Budgell protested in vain to Curll against what he declared to be an invasion of his private affairs. In an advertisement of the pamphlet inserted in the *Daily Journal* (September 20, 1733), Curll printed several letters relating to the affair and menacingly concluded with this open letter:

'To Mr. Budgell

Sir,

I will shortly shew the World who best understands the ARTS of Imposing upon and Cheating both Private Persons and the Publick.

This Affair between YOU and I, shall (in your own most elegant Phrase) MAKE A GOOD DEAL OF NOISE, before I have done with you. I expect your True Answer.

E. CURLL.'

Two other pamphlets, issued by another bookseller, completed the exposure: the first, which was obviously based on information from the nephew, revealed some very odd circumstances in connection with the will; the second, the work of one William Webster, took the form of an ironical defence and was written with malicious effectiveness. The first pamphlet bore the title *A Copy of the Will of Dr. Matthew Tindal, with An Account of What pass'd concerning the Same, Between Mrs. Lucy Price, Eustace Budgell Esq. and Mr. Nicholas Tindal.* It showed that the first news of the uncle's death was received by Nicholas Tindal in a letter from Mrs. Price of Gray's Inn ('relict of Judge Price'), who wrote that 'having been many years intimately acquainted, he thought fit to repose the greatest confidence in me. He hath put his Will in my hands, and, as you are one of the Executors I thought myself obliged to give you this notice.' The pamphlet went on to state that the nephew had been assured by several eyewitnesses that Dr. Tindal had lately made a will appointing him as sole heir, and only five weeks before his death his uncle had told him that he had left him everything but his manuscripts. It seemed strange to him that he had not been informed of his uncle's illness; he was told by 'the woman of the house' that Dr. Tindal had sent for him, 'but the letter had not been sent to the Post-house.'

'Upon this, Mr. Tindal in company with a Friend goes to Mr. Budgell's (whose house was very near to the Doctor's lodgings) where, after some general discourse concerning the Doctor, Mr. Budgell takes him aside and tells him, "that his Uncle had entertain'd a great value for him, whether on account of his personal Merits, or for his Works, he could not say; and, as a mark of it, had committed to his care the publishing of the Manuscripts." Adding, "that out of a generous Compassion for his Misfortunes, and in consideration of the Trouble he might undergo in printing his Papers, the Doctor, he believ'd, had moreover left him a very HANDSOME LEGACY, which (continues he) let it be what you will, you are not to reckon as a loss, for you must know, your Uncle was of opinion there will be very quickly a change in the Ministry, and from Something he saw in me, imagined, I should be, as he was pleased to express it, a GREAT MAN, and therefore has laid me under the strongest obligations, when such a change happens, to provide for you and your family." '

This rambling explanation only confirmed the nephew's suspicion that there was something peculiar about the will and that the failure to inform him of his uncle's illness had been deliberate. But more disquieting circumstances were to be revealed. The will was in the handwriting of Mrs. Price and had been witnessed by Budgell's footman and the landlady. When the strong box was opened it was found that it contained only a bond for £1,000 which Dr. Tindal had lent to Budgell and various items to the value of £60. Asked for information about the financial position, the bankers declared that for many years Dr. Tindal had not been possessed of more than £1,900 in stock and that on June 2, 1732, they had sold £1,000 of this and paid the sum in bank notes to Dr. Tindal and that later they had sold a further £800 of stock and heard him say that he was lending the money on bond. Thus, as the writer of the pamphlet pointed out, 'the Will was made upon the Supposition that the Doctor was worth more than Two thousand pounds. . . What ARTS were used to induce an old man, naturally very close, to lend his ALL upon BOND, or what other methods were taken to get possession of his effects, is a secret, which must be left to Mrs. Price and Time to discover.'[1]

[1] I have not been able to trace any statement made by Mrs. Price to justify the rôle she played, nor any suggestion that she personally benefited. She was a judge's widow and therefore a

A footnote to the pamphlet suggested that Dr. Tindal had removed from Gray's Inn to Cold Bath Fields at the instance of Budgell, and that by management certain of his friends were prevented from seeing him or if they gained admittance from talking to him.

The second pamphlet, *A Vindication of Eustace Budgell, Esq. from some Aspersions thrown upon him in a late Pamphlet,* began by restating the charges against Budgell with the precision of a legal indictment (ostensibly as a preface to the task of clearing his name) and gave emphasis to an allegation that he had planned to make a fraudulent claim upon the estate by suggesting that he had not received the £1,000 due to him under the bond. When he was confronted with the evidence that the bank notes had been traced to him, Budgell said that Dr. Tindal had lent him the sum but that he had repaid it. The pamphleteer continued, with pretended indignation:

'Nothing appearing to disprove it, it is unreasonable to question Mr. Budgell's Veracity. The utmost that can be made of this weighty Business, is, that Mr. Budgell has a treacherous Memory. . . That a Gentleman and a Philosopher; a Gentleman of so clear a Reputation; and a Philosopher of such sound Principles of Virtue and Honour; that a Disciple of so Godlike a Master, with the Impressions of his Master's divine Precepts and Behaviour in his last and most affecting Moments so strong upon him; to say, that Mr. Budgell in such Circumstances could be guilty of, or not confess, such dishonourable

woman of social standing, and a prompt and firm declaration by her would have carried weight. Her name was coupled with Budgell's as co-forger, but the wounding attacks made by Grub Street did not include any hint that they were more than friends. The silence of Mrs. Price throughout long weeks of reiterated accusation must have been interpreted as strong presumptive evidence that the will was a forgery.

Practices, is morally impossible, and therefore highly incredible.

'But there is one Circumstance which shews that the whole Charge is plainly the Effect of Malice. In this Libel Mr. Budgell is accused of Vanity; and a Person that can say that of Mr. Budgell, may say any Thing.'

The writer concluded: 'I think I have taken the Sting out of this poisonous Wasp who has endeavour'd to hurt an innocent Bee.' A small-type 'Advertisement' that followed made plain the real intent of the pamphlet: 'Whereas there was a Counterfeit Defence of Mr. Budgell published last Saturday in a Weekly Paper called the Bee, with the Intent to Expose the Gentleman, this is to assure the Publick, that the only genuine Defence that ever has been, or ever will be, printed, is published by Mr. Cooper in Ivy-Lane.' Both pamphlets carried the imprint of 'T. Cooper, at the *Globe* in Ivy-Lane.'

These pamphlets alone were sufficient to destroy the reputation of Eustace Budgell; their effect was powerfully reinforced by a sustained attack in the columns of the *Grub Street Journal*. Every detail of the affair was brought under hard scrutiny in a series of articles spread over several months. The longest of these articles, printed on November 22, 1733, occupied over a page (the *Grub Street Journal* was a four-page weekly). Two damaging points made in this attack were: (a) Since, according to Budgell, Dr. Tindal wrote several letters in his own hand shortly before his death, why was not the will (a short document) in his own handwriting? (b) As Dr. Tindal was still 'in full possession of his great natural parts' and read the will five or six times—again according to Budgell—why having correctly signed his name with one L did he fail to notice that it was misspelt with two l's in the body of the will?

Budgell defended himself at great length in the pages of the *Bee* against this trial by pamphlet and newspaper.

Week after week for some months his apparently long-suffering readers were confronted with letters and articles on the affair of the will: in several issues a quarter of the magazine was devoted to the subject. Throughout he spelt Dr. Tindal's name with two l's. Budgell asserted that he lent him the £1,000 to get his pamphlet on a good footing and said that the bond could run for four years. 'Mr. Budgell said, he could not be sure of repaying him at the End of that Time. The Doctor replied with a Smile, that perhaps, there might be no Occasion for him ever to repay it.' One article ended with an account of an assault (apparently only verbal) upon Budgell in Fleet Street by Edmund Curll's son: 'The Fellow set upon him in the open Street, by giving him the most abusive Language he could possibly invent; he gathered the Mob about Mr. Budgell, and told them, that was the Rogue who was the Scribbler of the BEE, the Villain that wrote against the Government, and the Fellow that had forged the Will.'

The issue for December 1, 1733, contained a 'Letter from a Friend,' headed with the assurance, 'The following LETTER is Genuine.' One can imagine the sardonic comment of Grub Street on this assurance, especially when it was discovered that the letter mainly consisted of a defence of Budgell along familiar lines. The writer began: 'I am an idle Man; (that is), engaged in no Business; I read most Things that come out and will bear to be read: Among our modern Writings none have pleased me more than those of Mr. Budgell; and from liking his Writings first, I am at last come to love the Man. . . Good God! What has this poor Gentleman suffered! . . .' The first hint of legal action is seen in this heading to a note in the issue for March 22, 1734: 'Some Account of a very extraordinary Cause which is commenced in Doctors Commons. . . with a Design if possible to set aside the Will of the late Dr. Tindall.'

In several issues the *Bee* gave prominence to an offer of prize medals to those who sent in the best Latin and

English verses in honour of the memory of Dr. Tindal. In one of the letters printed in his magazine Budgell represented himself as the guardian—the very necessary guardian—of the dead man's manuscripts. 'I have received numberless Cautions to take care of the Doctor's manuscripts, and some intimation that there was a Design laid to seize and suppress such Writings as he has left behind him. I hope and believe that no such infamous Design was ever laid: However, *A burnt Child dreads the Fire*. It is certain my own Papers have been twice seized and rifled in the most scandalous and notorious Manner.' The dark references by this unhappy man to persecution by the authorities and others, a recurring feature in his pamphlets and in his contributions to the *Bee*, make painful reading. The following, one of the most characteristic, must be limited to its preamble: 'We live in an Age, in which few but the Rich and the Powerful have had any Regard paid to them: yet even in this Age, when I was hardly got out of a Prison, where I had been unjustly confined for four years. . . when I had Law-Suits upon Law-Suits multiplied upon me, and was daily worried by a certain Pack of Blood-Hounds in the shape of Attornies. . .'

The charge of forgery was never legally proved. Somehow Budgell, mentally disordered but still a master of evasion, kept his enemies at bay for four years, and it is not pleasant to contemplate his wretched existence during these four years. He was now completely discredited, and there is no evidence that he was engaged in any literary work after the suspension of the *Bee*.

Apparently there came a moment when he saw that he could no longer evade formal retribution—the loss of his magazine, the final collapse of what had been not unworthy ambitions and the humiliations inflicted upon him by Grub Street were in themselves a crushing penalty for his crime—and he decided to put an end to the nightmare that his life had become. The last chapter was pathetically chronicled in these newspaper reports:

'Wednesday Morning, about 11 o'clock, over-against King's Stairs at Tower-Wharf, the body of a Man was seen floating in the Water, which was soon brought to Shore by a Waterman; and by Circumstances is believed to be the Gentleman who took that Boat last Week at Dorset Stairs, and said he was going to Greenwich, but jump'd out of the Boat at London Bridge, and was seen no more, leaving a Silver-hilted Sword behind him. On searching his Pockets there was found a Gold Watch, and some Money; as also a Paper with these Words, The Bearer hereof, Eustace Budgell, Esq., is my Secretary, and signed ORRERY. The body was convey'd to a House, till Advice was sent to his Friends.'

> *The Country Journal: or, The Craftsman,*
> May 14, 1737.

'On Thursday night the Coroner's Inquest sat on the body of Eustace Budgell, Esq: and after examining the waterman out of whose boat he threw himself, the watermen who took him up, &c. brought in their verdict *Lunacy.* He appear'd very much disorder'd for a day or two before he drowned himself. His servant maid, the night before hid his sword, which used to lay under his pillow, to prevent his attempting his life. As he went out, he said he should not come home any more, and talk'd very wildly. His maid, who watch'd him, saw him take a coach in Hatton-garden, and took the number of the coach: when he came to Holborn, he discharg'd that coach, and took another, in which he drove to Dorset-stairs, where he was seen stooping several times, and 'tis supposed fill'd his pockets with stones, and then took water, &c.—He had about him, when taken up, a Bank-bill of 71*l.* another of 50*l.* a note of Sir Francis Child's for 20*l.* 20 guineas in money, and a gold watch.—'Tis said

that he expected an execution would enter his house the
next day; and that he had a cause to come on at Westminster Hall, which gave him great uneasiness.—He left
in his escrutore a short scrap of a Will, wrote a day or
two before, importing, that he left to his natural daughter
Ann Eustace (a girl of about eleven years of age)[1] all his
personal estate. [Added to the report was this quotation
from the *London Daily Post:* "This Cause at Westminster
Hall, we hear, related to the late Dr. Tindal's Will."] '
Grub Street Journal, May 19, 1737.

On his desk Eustace Budgell had left a sheet of paper
bearing this justification of his last decision:

> 'What Cato did and Addison approved
> Cannot be wrong.'

But better known to posterity are the lines that Pope
inserted in his *Epistle to Dr. Arbuthnot:*

> 'Let Budgell charge low Grub Street on his quill,
> And write whate'er he pleased—except his will.'

[1] She later became an actress at Drury Lane.

The First Columnist

*

WHEN things were going well with Dr. John Hill—in later life self-styled Sir John Hill, on the strength of an honour conferred by the King of Sweden—he was to be seen in London riding in his splendid chariot, a style of carriage much favoured in the eighteenth century for its elegance and genteelness. The first of these successful phases came in the early seventeen-fifties, when he was about thirty-five and reputed to be earning £1,500 a year as author and as chief contributor to a London daily newspaper: he can be ranked as the first columnist, in the sense that he was the first writer of a regular signed newspaper feature.[1]

This spectacle of worldly success was enough by itself to provoke the dark envy of Grub Street, but Dr. Hill was so prodigal in his disclosures of his fashionable life and referred so grandly to 'My Domestics' and 'My equipage' that he stirred up a hornets' nest of wits into furious attack. For the rest of his life, including the last phase when he was probably the most prosperous quack of his time and had a town house and a country house, the wits followed his progress with malicious attentiveness and have bequeathed us a sort of profile of Dr. Hill in epigrams.

Apothecary, botanist, actor, scholar, farce-writer, doctor, editor, author, quack, man of fashion—this is a bare summary of the many rôles he played. Christopher Smart, the poet, whom he had grossly attacked, labelled him 'Wit, moralist, quack, harlequin and beau;' and harle-

---

[1] The term appears to have originated in the United States early in this century, but did not come into general use until about the nineteen-thirties.

quin seems not inappropriate after a survey of his fantastic career—with its ludicrous moments—and his mischievous activity as a journalist. Hill had also the reputation, not unjustified, of being one of the greatest liars of his time.

But more is to be discovered in the career of Dr. Hill than a shabby harlequinade, a series of profitable impostures: there is a residue of genuine achievement, evidence that if he had not been eager for money at all costs he might have made an honourable name for himself as an authority on botany. Dr. Johnson summed him up very fairly in his reply to George the Third, who asked him what he thought of Dr. Hill. Johnson answered that he was an ingenious man but had no veracity. Notwithstanding, he was a very curious observer, and if he had been content to tell the world no more than he knew, he might have been a very considerable man. Johnson might have added—but never a likeable one.

Son of a clergyman, Hill was born in 1716 at Peterborough. At an early age he was apprenticed to an apothecary, and on completion of his apprenticeship he set up for himself by opening a small shop in St. Martin's Lane, London. This was not very profitable, and he took up the study of botany with a view to supplementing his income and was engaged by the Duke of Richmond and Lord Petre to arrange their gardens and their collections of dried plants. Stimulated no doubt by the contemporary fame of Linnaeus, he conceived a project that would have made a useful contribution to botanical knowledge. His plan was to travel all over England in search of the rarest plants, specimens of which, dried by a special process that he had invented and accompanied by descriptive letterpress, he would publish by subscription. But the idea was not a success and he now went on the stage. Acting was so little his forte, however, that it is recorded that he did not even impress in the part of the apothecary in *Romeo and Juliet*—but nevertheless a few years later he boldly wrote a book entitled *The Actor: A treatise on the Art of Playing.*

Hill took up again the business of apothecary, with a shop in James Street, Covent Garden, and devoted part of his time to literature. He wrote the libretto of *Orpheus, an English Opera,* which he sent to John Rich, who refused it but in the following year produced Theobald's *Orpheus and Eurydice*—the provocation for the first of Hill's many literary quarrels. The publication of his translation of Theophrastus' history of gems in 1746 marked the turning point in his career. In the same year the first number of the *British Magazine* was issued, with Hill as editor.[1] People were now beginning to talk about him; he gained (but presently lost) the friendship of members of the Royal Society, who introduced him to authors; publishers sought his work. In this year, too, appeared his *History of Drugs.* There were dozens of books to follow in the next thirty years. Some were little more than rubbishy pamphlets and others were frankly vulgar, but one or two were substantial works, notably *A General Natural History* (three volumes) and *The Vegetable System* (26 volumes).

A diploma in medicine from the University of St. Andrew's served to consolidate his improved social position, and the fact that he was handsome and well turned out also contributed: he had now become a man of fashion and was to be seen regularly at Ranelagh, the theatres and Society routs. The Bedford Coffee House in

[1] The bound volumes of the *British Magazine* were among the books that the British Museum lost by enemy action in the Second World War. Mr. Walter Graham, in *English Literary Periodicals* (Nelson, New York, 1930), gives this description of the magazine: 'It was more elaborately illustrated than its predecessors, and its contents were of a more general entertaining nature, although instruction as well as amusement was one of its objects. . . Altogether, the *British Magazine* was more like modern magazines than any of its forerunners.'

Covent Garden—frequented by Hogarth, Fielding and other celebrities of the arts—was the centre of his activities, and as he emerged from his chariot on arrival there he made a picture of foppish impressiveness.

When the *British Magazine* was discontinued at the end of 1750 he almost immediately found the new post that was to make him the most discussed journalist of his day. For two years from March, 1751, he wrote a daily letter, under the signature of 'The Inspector,' for the two-page *London Advertiser, and Literary Gazette* (subsequently retitled the *London Daily Advertiser*)—a feature that the elder D'Israeli later characterised as 'a light scandalous chronicle all the week with a seventh-day sermon.' Hill promised to give accounts of 'the Polite World, and their Entertainments. . . which have never yet appeared as Part of the Intelligence of the Day: These we shall search after among the Assemblies of the Great, and at the Amusement of the Gay; at Routs and Assemblies, at Masquerades and Ridottoes, at Operas and at the Playhouses, at *Ranelagh*. . .'

Dr. Hill's article usually occupied about two and a half out of the three columns on the front page. It was the time of his greatest success: he was making £1,500 a year, an extraordinary income for a writer in those days, and he was finding his daily article a congenial vehicle for publicising himself and for exercising his talent for mischievous writing and—according to his multiplying enemies—for downright lying. He more than once confessed to falsehoods and this unexpected frankness produced the retort:

'What Hill does one day say, he the next does deny,
And candidly tells you,—'tis all a damned lie:
Dear Doctor,—this candour from you is not wanted,
For why should you own it?—'tis taken for granted.'

One victim of his malice, an Irishman named Mounte-

fort Brown, kicked him, pulled off his wig and caned him
at one of his favourite resorts—Ranelagh. The incident
was portrayed with much relish in a contemporary print,
and general report suggested that Hill showed cowardice
on this notorious occasion. He took to his bed and printed
his own version of the affair after his usual 'Inspector'
article (May 7, 1752). According to this he had received
a letter from Brown, who 'fancied I had drawn his character in the Inspector on Thursday last.'

'Last Night he came up to me in the Room at Ranelagh.
He was beginning to talk loud, and I had notice of a
Party being about him by some Persons bidding him put
on his Hat, which he held off while he spoke to me. I
desired him not to disturb the Company, to speak in the
Garden. I was alone: Those who had been with him in
the Room followed us out. Soon after we were without
the Door, some Person seized on my Neck behind, and in
a Moment after three others held me by the Collar, while
Mr. Brown was drawing his Sword. I called to the Master
of the House, who was fortunately passing by. . . Officers
were procured, into whose Hands Mr. Brown was delivered, but as they were carrying him off he was rescued
from them by the same Party. Warrants are now out
against six of these, and diligent Search is making after
them, in order to bring them to Justice.'

Writing two days later, under the caption 'The Author
of the Inspector to the Public,' Hill painted this lurid
picture of his condition: 'The Physician who attends me
has confirmed my own Opinion, by declaring, the Hurt I
have received is not without Danger. The Stream of Life
which I lose in greater and greater Quantities, brings the
King of Silence toward me with hastier Steps. . .' Critical
readers of the paper must have been sceptical about the
gravity of the injuries when they noted that 'The Inspector' was still able, despite his weakened condition, to

produce something like 1,400 words a day. When, rather oddly, he told the story of his having once given a beating to a man he called Mario, a wit penned this neat retort:

'To beat one man, great Hill was fated.
What man? A man whom he created.'

Brown the Irishman, otherwise obscure, gained a modest immortality by the manner of his revenge. Other victims of Hill's scurrilous pen were well-known personalities—among them David Garrick, Henry Fielding and Christopher Smart—and they retaliated with wit and vigour. Because a farce that he had written was hissed off the stage at Covent Garden Hill vented his rage on Garrick, under whose management it had been presented. The reply made by Garrick to these spiteful attacks was terse and caustic:

'For physic and farces, his equal there scarce is;
His farces are physic, his physic a farce is.'

Dr. Hill had not yet exhausted his spite. He wrote a pamphlet entitled *To David Garrick, Esq; the Petition of I in behalf of herself and her Sisters,* in which he accused the actor of misusing *i* and *u* in such words as firm and virtue, pronouncing them furm and vurtue. But Garrick once more showed his readiness at turning an epigram to fit the occasion:

'If 'tis true, as you say, that I've injured a letter,
I'll change my note soon, and I hope for the better.
May the right use of letters, as well as of men,
Hereafter be fix'd by the tongue and the pen.
Most devoutly I wish they may both have their due,
And that *I* may never be mistaken for *U*.'

The clash with Fielding arose from the mock war between 'the Forces under Sir Alexander Drawcansir and the Army of Grub Street' which the novelist good-humouredly, but ponderously, described in the first issue of his twice-a-week paper the *Covent-Garden Journal* ('By Sir Alexander Drawcansir, Censor of Great Britain'). In the second article, which was lighter in treatment, Fielding facetiously paid off his score against Smollett, who had made a vulgar allusion (without naming him) to his second marriage to his 'cook-wench.' He also made a mild and glancing reference to Dr. Hill. Various newspapers joined in the Paper War, as it was called, and taking it seriously developed the affair into what two centuries later seems merely a ridiculous and boring squabble.[1] Hill entered into the spirit of the jest at first, but in a subsequent article alleged that Fielding had told him that 'he held the present set of Writers in the utmost Contempt, and that in his Character of Drawcansir he should treat them in the most unmerciful Manner. . . He proceeded to mention a Conduct which would be, he said, useful to both: this was the amusing of our readers with a Mock-fight; giving Blows that would not hurt, and sharing the Advantage in Silence. I hold the public in too great Respect to trifle with it in so disingenuous a Manner. . . Whom I slighted as an Associate, I cannot fear as an Adversary. . . I am sorry to insult the departed Spirit of a Living Author. . . I drop a Tear. . . when I see the Author of Joseph Andrews doting in the *Covent-garden Journal*.' He suggested that Fielding was anxious to continue the Paper War indefinitely for the money that might be in it. Fielding was so stung by this unexpected attack that he descended to the Grub Street level in his rejoinder:

[1] A full account of the Paper War, together with the text of the journal itself, can be found in *The Covent-Garden Journal*, edited by Gerard Edward Jensen (Oxford University Press, 1915).

'It being reported to the General that a HILL must be levelled before the Bedford Coffee House could be taken, Orders were given accordingly; but this was afterwards found to be a Mistake, a second Express assuring us, that this HILL was only a little paultry DUNGHILL, and had long before been levelled with the Dirt. The General was then informed of a Report which had been spread by *his Lowness* the Prince of Billingsgate, in the Grub-Street Army, that his Excellency had proposed by secret Treaty with that Prince, to carry on the War only in Appearance, against him, and so to betray the common Cause; upon which his Excellency said with a smile, If the Betrayer of a private Treaty could ever deserve the least credit, yet his Lowness here must proclaim himself either a Liar, or a Fool. . . The General added. . . that *his Lowness* was not only among the meanest of those who ever drew a Pen, but was absolutely the vilest fellow that ever wore a Head.'

Hill's next onslaught was the publication in two successive issues of the *London Daily Advertiser* (January 10 and 11, 1752) of a vulgar and stupid burlesque on Fielding as a magistrate with the caption 'The Genuine Trial of Mary, late Cook-Maid to Sir Simon Pride, before the worshipful Mr. Justice Feeler, for lying a-bed in a Morning, &c., &c.' (Mary was the Christian name of Fielding's second wife, who had been his first wife's maid.)

Another of Hill's numerous quarrels was with Christopher Smart, and he devised a crafty method of striking at the poet, though Grub Street was not deceived by this guile. He published on August 13, 1752, the first (and only) number of a paper called the *Impertinent,* in which he abused Smart; and in a subsequent 'Inspector' article he announced, with hypocritical pleasure, that the paper had been a failure: 'It will not be easy to say too much in favour of that Candour, which has rejected and despised a Piece that cruelly and unjustly attacked Mr. Smart.' By exciting curiosity he secured publicity for his paper of a day. Nevertheless he made further attacks on the poet in two 'Inspector' articles published in the following December.

Smart's satirical reply, published in 1753 under the title of *The Hilliad*, is bitingly effective. It is tempting to quote at length, but this sample will indicate its quality:

> 'O thou, whatever name delights thine ear,
> Pimp! Poet! Puffer! 'Pothecary! Play'r!
> Whose baseless fame by vanity is buoy'd,
> Like the huge earth self-center'd in the void,
> Accept one partner thy own worth t'explore,
> And in thy praise be singular no more.'

'The Inspector' added a then small (but influential) section of the community to his enemies by ridiculing scientific men. The antiquarians were contemptuously described as medal-scrapers and antediluvian knife-grinders, the conchologists as cockleshell merchants and the naturalists as compilers of pompous histories of sticklebacks and cockchafers. Later he sought to become a Fellow of the Royal Society, but not surprisingly he was unable to obtain the requisite three signatures of recommendation. Scientists could not, in any case, have any respect for the author of *Lucina sine Concubitu* (1750), 'a letter humbly addressed to the Royal Society' that contained a farrago of obscene nonsense. The sub-title was in English that is too explicit for twentieth-century ears. Briefly, the pamphlet claimed to establish 'by most Incontestable Evidence, Drawn from Reason and Practice' that human parthenogenesis was a fact.

Hill was never a man to let a slight pass without notice. In a preface to a book that he produced in 1751, *A Review of the Work of the Royal Society of London; containing Animadversions on such of the Papers as des-*

erve Particular Observation, he said that it had been 'very freely asserted, that he put himself to the Ballot for Choice, and been rejected by a great Majority.' On the contrary, he had always been 'determinately and immoveably on the Side of avoiding what these Gentlemen suppose an Honour.'

1099399

'They seem to be in a Confederacy against Men of polite Genius, noble Thought, and diffusive Learning; and chuse into their Assemblies such as have no Pretence to Wisdom, but Want of Wit; or to natural knowledge, but Ignorance of every thing else.'

His failure to gain admission to the Royal Society long rankled in his mind. Ten years later he wrote an eighteen-page pamphlet, *Some Projects Recommended to the Society for the Encouragement of Arts, Manufactures, and Commerce,* by 'The Inspector, Proposed F.R.S.' (which suggests a parallel with the Indian student's 'Failed B.A.'), with this preface:

'Gentlemen, my Vanity is not in the least mortifyed by the Repulse I received, when I was proposed to be elected as a Member of your Society. . . My Opponents all came from one Quarter to gratify their Resentment. I forgive them freely. They had received great Provocation from me: For I had dragged into the open Light, their Ignorance and Dulness, which had so long skulked under the Veil of Science and Philosophy. . . Permit me to lay before you some Projects, which will be of excellent Service to our Country, and will redound to your Honour.

The proposals outlined included suggestions for the tanning of human skins for various uses; the encouragement of native singers, and the purchase of about twenty acres to be converted into a botanic garden ('the Care and Management of which I will undertake with a handsome Gratuity'). The first project is treated in a manner that now reads like a page out of a satire. The pamphlet *may* have been ironical, but the workings of Hill's mind were so extraordinary that nothing seemed too fantastic for him to advance seriously.

His books (over 70 in number) dealt with such diverse subjects as *The Conduct of a Married Life, Observations on the Greek and Roman Classics* and *Cautions Against the Immoderate Use of Snuff;* most of them reflect his interest in botany and medicine. The British Museum copy of his *Old Man's Guide to Health and Longer Life* is the sixth edition, 'corrected and enlarged.' It is a 50-page book consisting largely of platitudes, together with recommendations on diet that would sound less grotesque in the eighteenth century than they do today. For example: 'Let the breakfast be a yolk of an egg, beaten up with half a pint of asses milk, and a quarter of an ounce of conserve of roses; and as supper veal broth nearly boiled to a jelly. For afternoon let him take half a pint of asses milk alone. . .'

In a 21-page biography published, at the instance of his widow, after his death, under the title *Short Account of the Life, Writings, and Character of the late Sir John Hill, M.D., Acad.Reg. Scient.Burd etc. Soc.*, appears this reference to his literary labours:

'His numerous works, upon a vast variety of subjects, while they procured him the patronage of the best and greatest Personages in this, as well as in other countries, at the same time raised up a host of foes, enemies to him as well as to knowledge. These did not fail to make use of every engine malevolence could invent, to depreciate the character and the works of a man, whom they saw, with regret, every way so far their superior.'

Among his patrons was Lord Bute, at whose request

Hill embarked on his most ambitious work—*The Vegetable System,* in 26 volumes, with 1,600 copperplate engravings illustrating 26,000 different plants drawn from nature. Lord Bute also obtained for him the post of superintendent of the Royal Gardens at Kew, but the appointment was not confirmed.

This was the period of Hill's greatest fashionable success. His second wife was a sister of Lord Ranelagh, and it was through this marriage that he became acquainted with the leaders of Society and gained the patronage of Bute. Not everyone found this social recruit acceptable. In a letter dated February 15, 1759, Horace Walpole indignantly commented on his discovery that Hill had been writing in his defence against the *Critical Review.* 'They tell me nobody can suspect my being privy to it: but there is an intimacy affected that I think will deceive many—and yet I must be the most arrogant fool living, if I could know and suffer anybody to speak of me in that style. For God's sake, do all you can for me, and publish my abhorrence. Today I am told that it is that puppy Doctor Hill, who has chosen to make war with the Magazines through my sides. I could pardon any abuse, but I never can forgive this *friendship.*'

Dr. Hill's great botanical work occupied him from 1759 to 1775 and involved him in considerable financial loss, but it brought him as compensation an honour which he exploited to the utmost. The posthumous biography relates that he was 'particularly patronised by the countenance of various foreign Princes, from several of whom he received many rich and curious presents. But, the most distinguished honour which the Author received, was that which was conferred on him by that great admirer of Genius and Learning, the present King of Sweden. . . His Majesty wrote a letter to our Author, with his own hand, acquainting him, that, as a testimony of his regard, he meant to invest him with the illustrious Order of Vasa.' He received this honour in 1774 and

thereafter assumed the style of Sir John Hill.[1] His other
honours were listed as 'Member of the Imperial Academy'
and 'Fellow of the Royal Academy of Sciences at Bor-
deaux,' and he was a justice of the peace for Westminster.

It was not his literary work that enabled Dr. Hill in his
later years to maintain his fine chariot, his town house in
St. James's Street and his country house. He continued to
produce books of various types, but he could no longer
rely on his pen to bring him the ample income that had
rewarded him in his 'Inspector' days. The simple explanation of his affluence was that he had become a quack on
the grand scale. In a pamphlet on *The Virtue of British
Herbs,* illustrated with plates giving their Linnaean
names, he had spoken highly of the medicinal qualities
of his favourite herbs; now he produced herb medicines
which were soon bringing him large profits—among them
'essence of waterdock,' 'pectoral balsam of honey' and
'tincture of valerian.' The herbs were cultivated in his
extensive gardens at Bayswater (on the site now covered
by Lancaster Gate), where he had his country house.
The wits of Grub Street were once more stirred into
activity. As one wrote:

'Thou essence of dock, and valerian, and sage,
At once the disgrace and the pest of the age,
The worst that we wish thee, for all thy crimes,
Is to take thy own physic, and read thy own rhymes.'

Another writer saw a way to give a neat twist to the
idea:

'The wish must be in form reversed,
To suit the doctor's crimes,
For, if he takes his physic first,
He'll never read his rhymes.'

[1] A few years earlier William Chambers, the architect of Somer-
set House and other well-known buildings, received the Order of
the Polar Star from the Swedish King, and *by permission* of King
George III adopted the equivalent British title.

One of his medicinal preparations was 'tincture of bardana,' described as an invaluable specific for gout. When Hill died of (it was alleged) that complaint in 1775—at the age of 59—it was inevitable that a wit should compose his epitaph.

> 'Poor Doctor Hill is dead! Good lack!'
> 'Of what disorder?' 'An attack
> Of gout.' 'Indeed! I thought that he
> Had found a wondrous remedy.'
> 'Why, so he had, and when he tried,
> He found it true—the doctor died!'

The Strange Case of
the Murdered Editor

*

IMAGINE that one night the editor of a London morning newspaper is murdered in his office by a masked man and that the next day neither his own journal nor any other paper makes any reference to the crime. . . The first supposition appears melodramatic and the second grotesquely improbable.

But consider what happened in the office of the *Morning Post* one night late in 1832—or was it early in 1833? For this detail, like so many others of this strange chapter of journalistic history, is a vital fact that has eluded a prolonged investigation into the mystery of the death of Nicholas Byrne, editor of the *Morning Post* for thirty years. Not only did this major crime go unreported, but it is without a date in the precise sense of that word.

Brief mention of this crime that so curiously escaped contemporary record can be found in several works published in the present century. Reginald Lucas, in *Lord Glenesk and the 'Morning Post,'*[1] made this reference: 'In the early days of the nineteenth century, when political life was full of violence, one editor of the Morning Post, Eugenius Roche, had been imprisoned for libel, whilst another, Nicholas Byrne, was destined to be assassinated in his office as the penalty of his outspoken Toryism.' The *Encyclopædia Britannica*, in its article on 'Newspapers,' states that the *Morning Post* 'always maintained a tradition of vigorous and unblenching criticism, and Nicholas Byrne, the editor-owner who succeeded Daniel Stuart, was murdered in his office as the result of

[1] Alston Rivers, 1910.

an article which had given offence.' The source of these
and similar references to the death of Byrne is revealed
by Mr. Wilfrid Hindle in *The Morning Post: 1772-1937*[1]
as the centenary issue of the paper, and after summar-
ising the account that appears there Mr. Hindle comments: 'As the criminal was never brought to justice, the
motive of the crime is not certainly known; it is possible
it was political.' Here is the relevant passage from the
Morning Post of November 2, 1872:

'For many years the *Morning Post* was the stanch *(sic)*
and consistent advocate and supporter of the Pitt Admin-
istration. The then proprietor, Mr. Nicholas Byrne, a
gentleman of independent fortune, and the descendant
of an old Tory family, was the intimate friend of the great
statesman. Party feeling ran very high in those days, and
Mr. Byrne wrote vigorously and persistently in defence
of the Minister, and as a matter of course brought upon
himself the hostility of his political opponents, public as
well as private. The uncompromising firmness of the
Morning Post on many remarkable occasions has become
a matter of contemporary history. . . The life of the
proprietor was twice attempted, and on the second occasion with lamentable success. One winter's night, or
rather morning, nearly forty years ago, when Mr. Byrne
was sitting alone in his office, a man entered unchal-
lenged from the street, and made his way to his room.
He wore a crape mask, and rushing upon his victim
stabbed him twice with a dagger. Mr. Byrne, though
mortally wounded, gave the alarm, and managed to
follow his assailant to the street, but he escaped in the
darkness of the night, and was never brought to justice.'

A comment is called for on the first part of this extract,
which by its telescoping of thirty years' history gives a
misleading impression. Pitt died in 1806, a quarter of a

[1] Routledge, 1937.

century before Byrne, and if the cause of the latter's death was political vengeance it arose from controversy of a much later date.

This short account, published forty years after the event, contains everything that is known about the attack on Byrne, and as far as can be ascertained after exhaustive search which I have made of contemporary newspapers and periodicals it is *the first and only* report of the crime that ever appeared in print—and as will later be seen it is strangely inaccurate and must have been written from hearsay. Certainly it could not have been written by a surviving member of Byrne's staff, unless his memory had seriously failed.

But before going further into the peculiar circumstances of this crime an endeavour must be made to fill in the background of Nicholas Byrne and his newspaper.

The numerous volumes of history, biography and social and political gossip covering the first third of the nineteenth century are richly peopled with celebrities and near-celebrities; a great deal has been written about editors of the period, including the predecessors and successors of Byrne in the editorial chair of the *Morning Post:* but though for thirty years he controlled what was then a prominent newspaper robustly engaged in political controversy, he has left hardly a trace in the annals of his times. The *Dictionary of National Biography,* generous on the whole in its allotment of space to prominent journalists, has no article on Byrne, though it contains a biography of his daughter-in-law, Julia C. Byrne (Mrs. W. Pitt Byrne), who is remembered as the author of books on social problems and several volumes of entertaining gossip. No encyclopædia has a biography of Byrne. The *Annual Register* (which printed a brief notice of the death of his son Charles) and the *Gentleman's Magazine,* both of which methodically recorded the deaths of well-known persons and gave much space in their obituary sections to other editors of the period who died before or after Byrne, did not even note the fact of his passing.

We know that Byrne was a friend of William Pitt and named his son after him, but I have not been able to trace any mention of him in the lives of Pitt, and the collection of the latter's correspondence at the Record Office does not include any letter to or from Byrne. We know that he was, in the old-fashioned phrase, a man of substance. He lived at 12, Lancaster Place, between the Strand and Waterloo Bridge, in a house forming part of a dignified terrace that was demolished after the First World War to make room for the tall office building called Brettenham House. The office of the *Morning Post* in Byrne's time was in the Strand and very close to Lancaster Place.

William Jerdan, editor of the *Literary Gazette*, who had worked under Byrne on the *Morning Post* early in the century, mentions him in his autobiography (1852) as an editor with 'a staff of high consideration'—but says nothing more. Alexander Andrews, in his *History of British Journalism* (1859), speaks of Byrne 'guiding the destinies of the *Morning Post*' and gives the names of some of his colleagues in 1812. H. R. Fox Bourne, author of *English Newspapers* (1887), the most complete of nineteenth-century histories of journalism, makes no mention of Byrne at all, though he has frequent references to the *Morning Post*.

What sort of a man was Byrne? I have not been able to trace a portrait of him, and the evidence upon which to form an impression of his personality is tantalisingly meagre. We know that he was a vigorous political controversialist, as will emerge when the character of the *Morning Post* under his direction comes to be examined; we know, as the wording of his will reveals, that he was a man of strong family affections; but of the personal and social side of his life we have but one brief glimpse, which appeared in Julia C. Byrne's *Gossip of the Century*.[1] After mentioning that John Parry, sen. (who became music critic of the *Morning Post* after Byrne's death) was a clever musician and that his son John (later to become a successful concert singer) showed a precocious taste for music, she gives this picture of musical evenings in Lancaster Place:

'His father being intimate with Mr. Nicholas Byrne, often dined at his house; on these occasions "Johnnie" used to be put on the table after dinner where he would delight the guests by the display of his talents, truly remarkable at this very early age. In after years, when he had become a celebrity, Mr. Byrne having remarked one day to his old friend John Parry *(père)* "Johnnie has become quite a lion now!" the old man answered, not without emotion, "Yes, Mr. Byrne; but I shall never forget that it was you who gave him his mane." '

In his will, dated August 22, 1829, Byrne, who was then a widower, made a bequest of £10,000 to 'my dear daughter Maria' and of £2,000 and a one-fourth interest in the *Morning Post* to 'my dear son Charles.'

'. . . And as to all the Rest residue and remainder of my real and personal estate of what nature kind quality or description soever I give devise and bequeath the same unto my dear beloved son William his heirs executors administrators and assigns for ever according to the nature or terms thereof respectively having the fullest confidence in the kind goodness and affection of his Heart that he will watch over and pay attention to the interest and comfort of my dear Maria his sister and I appoint him my said son William sole executor of this my last Will and Testament. . . '

[1] Ward and Downey, 1892.

In a codicil dated April 14, 1832, Byrne gave bitter expression to his dislike of the marriage that his daughter had contracted in the meantime and was harshly precise to ensure that her husband should have no benefit from the fresh—and reduced—provision that he made for her.

'I revoke the legacy of ten thousand pounds three per cent consols given by my said Will to my daughter Maria which I do in consequence of her having married against my wishes and in direct opposition to my most earnest entreaties and frequent and most serious remonstrances and instead thereof I bequeath to her the annual interest or dividends of the sum of Two thousand pounds three pounds per cent consols for her life such interest or dividends to be paid into her own hands only and her receipt for the same to be the only good discharge and she shall not charge assign or anticipate such interest or dividends or any part thereof and the same shall be free from the disposition controul *(sic)* intermeddling debts and engagements of her present and future husband. . .'

The *Gentleman's Magazine* of January, 1832, contained this announcement: 'January 11, 1832. At the Savoy, C. Thomson, esq., Attorney-gen. of St. Kitts, the eldest son of the late C. Thomson, esq., to Maria, only dau. of N. Byrne, esq., of Lancaster Place.' (The Savoy Chapel, with its small churchyard, is immediately behind Lancaster Place, and is now hemmed in by the Savoy Hotel, Brettenham House and other buildings.) Whatever the nature of Byrne's objection to the marriage, it had obviously nothing to do with the social and professional standing of her husband, and he waited until three months after the wedding before altering his will.

Before the will was proved Charles, the younger son, had died of cholera—one sorrow that Byrne was spared. William Pitt Byrne, the elder son, who married Julia Clara Busk in 1842, died in 1861. His widow survived him for thirty-three years, and a biographical notice in the *Athenæum* (April 7, 1894) stated: 'The early loss of a most devoted husband for a time threw a shadow over her life—William Pitt Byrne, son of the Byrne who had thrown new energies into the support of Pitt and the Tory cause in the *Morning Post,* one of the austerest writers journalism has ever known. The son distinguished himself at Trinity College, Cambridge; but his abilities, while they made him a delightful companion, rather unfitted him to deal with the business details of a great paper when its proprietorship devolved upon him. Consequently, when he won Julia Busk for his companion in life, the newspaper was cast aside, and only the agreeable associations which a newspaper connection supplies retained.'

An oddly designed memorial to William Pitt Byrne—a fountain in traditional style resting on a crude cairn-like base—was erected in Bryanston Square (where he lived) about two years after his death. St. Marylebone Vestry thought the design unsuitable, but since the fountain was on private property they decided to let it remain. The inscription, effusively comprehensive, includes a tribute to Nicholas Byrne. The memorial was erected by the friends of William Pitt Byrne after a design by his widow. It is now in a state of disrepair: the fountain no longer functions.

What kind of newspaper was the *Morning Post* under Nicholas Byrne? His thirty years of editorial control coincided with one of the most critical eras in British history—the last twelve years of the Napoleonic Wars, the violent post-war agitation that provoked the 'Six Acts,' and the culminating drama of the Reform Bill campaign. He took over a paper which in firm hands had made a vigorous recovery after a period of decline that had brought it almost into the gutter. Started in 1772 with solidly respectable business backing and edited for a time by the Rev. Henry Bate, the notorious 'Fighting Parson,' the *Morning Post* had many vicissitudes and eventually its circulation dropped to 350 and its reputation to zero. At this point—in 1795—it was sold for £600, this sum covering the copyright, a house and the plant. The purchaser, Daniel Stuart, was to reveal himself as an editor of genius: within eight years he had restored the prosperity of the *Morning Post* and made it one of the most influential journals of the age. He sold it in 1803 for £25,000.

Byrne, the new editor, was a zealous Pittite and then as throughout his journalistic career a passionate champion of law and order: a man of strong political convictions and rigid sympathies, who in later years was to find himself increasingly out of touch with the spirit of the age. His great mistake as an editor was to conduct the *Morning Post* as a servile party organ; its success under Stuart had been due to its well-known independence. But he lacked also another Stuart asset—the journalistic vision that never loses sight of the primary importance of producing a first-class newspaper. There is no parallel during the Byrne period to the enterprise in news collection that was to mark *The Times* under John Walter II, and it was not surprising that the rising fortunes of that by then independent journal coincided with a steady decline in the circulation of the *Morning Post*.

What critical readers found hard to stomach in later years was the slavish admiration for the Prince Regent that was frequently expressed in the *Morning Post*, and it was darkly recalled that at one time (1788) the Prince had been a part owner of the paper. During the trial of Queen Caroline in 1820 George IV (as the Prince Regent had now become) found one of his most ardent supporters in the *Post*, whose comment on the affair included a vulgar reference to 'the Queen and her three B's—the *Baron*—the *bath*—and the *bottle*.' Popular sympathies were with the Queen, and the attitude of the *Morning*

Post provoked a violent reprisal. Julia C. Byrne, in *Gossip of the Century,* gave this account of what happened:

'During the trial, the office of the *Morning Post* (then at 335 in the Strand) became the object of a furious attack by the mob, who collected in front of it, yelling like savages; they drew up before the facade a huge cart full of stones and brickbats with which they smashed all the windows they could reach and battered the walls. I have been told by Mr. Wm. Pitt Byrne (whose father, Mr. Nicholas Byrne, well known for his Tory principles, was then the sole proprietor of that journal) that he himself was in the office on the first floor, where everything was smashed, and was compelled to retreat into an office on the north side of the building for the protection of his life. One of the clerks received one of these missiles with some force on the shoulder, and was seriously injured.'

Towards the close of Byrne's editorship, concern about the weakness of the papers that supported them led the Tories to appoint a committee of ex-ministers to consider what could be done to improve the situation. It was decided that the *Morning Post* would have to b the principal organ of the party. After falling to less tha 2,000 in 1830—half of what it was in Stuart's day—the circulation had revived a little. Byrne agreed to improve his paper, and the party undertook to supply him with material. John Wilson Croker, a prime mover in the affair, accepted Byrne's view that it was not necessary to increase the size of the paper. 'I think it better as it is,' wrote Croker to Lord Lowther (February 21, 1831), 'and if we help him with good smart articles it will do very well.' But Lord Lowther, reviewing the position three months later, wrote to his father (May 7, 1831):

'We can make nothing of the *Morning Post.* Old Byrne

has a sale for his fashionable news, and we had authority to assist him with reporters and a Parisian correspondence, but he would neither delay his press nor give room for such intelligence. I conclude he knows his own trade better than we do, and that he would not risk the readers of fashionable news for the prospect of making his paper a more decided political one. He is civil enough in inserting leaders and letters, but it is a small establishment, and unless articles go early they cannot be inserted.'[1]

With the circulation now rising Byrne was wise not to risk any setback by overloading his journal with politics. In the last years of his life the *Morning Post* was a four-page paper, with occasional eight-page issues. A sampling of the leading articles on various topics during this period reveals the editor as frequently in aggressive mood, though one of his final comments on the Reform Bill, published on May 4, 1832 (the month that saw the climax of that great constitutional struggle), was comparatively restrained:

'We entreat the country and the peerage calmly to consider the miserable consequences that must follow from the formation of a democratic House of Commons— a House of Commons created by the votes and sympathising only with the passions of the lower classes, and estranged from the property and intelligence of the community. . . In this country democracy would be more extravagantly mischievous than in any other, from the enormous masses of capital we have to protect, and the protection of which is essential to the very being of our commercial system.'

A personal attack on a Radical orator appeared in the

[1] Lonsdale MSS. Quoted in *Politics and the Press: 1780-1850,* by Arthur Aspinall (Home and Van Thal, 1949).

Morning Post for October 1, 1832. This issue typified how sparing Byrne was in his editorial expenditure. A large part of the paper consisted of extracts from Home and Continental newspapers and periodicals: a two-column review of the current *Fraser's Magazine* mainly took the form of quotation. There was a good variety of news, ranging in size from half a column to the short paragraphs at the foot of columns that were a feature of all contemporary dailies. A report of the funeral of Sir Walter Scott occupied a third of a column. Police intelligence, a great stand-by of newspapers at that time, filled a column. A report of the election of the Lord Mayor of London occupied another column. It was punctuated with parenthetical notes in italics—*Laughter and hisses—Loud hisses—Great cheering—Tremendous cheering*. Commenting on this meeting, the first leading article was contemptuously triumphant:

'It will be seen by the report of the proceedings at the election of the Lord Mayor that the Radical Party in the City of London are at an incalculable discount. The fact of one of the leading orators of this party being put down by a spontaneous burst of indignation at Common Hall, the very citadel of its strength, or, what is still more humiliating, being rescued from this fate only by the intercession of the Lord Mayor Elect, speaks volumes. . . A few months ago an orator of this kidney might have attempted any thing at a Common Hall, however base or absurd, not only with impunity but with success.'

Byrne was violently opposed to Anglo-French intervention on the side of the Belgians in their struggle with the Dutch, and some of his hardest-hitting leaders were concerned with this subject. For example:

' "All men are liars." So said, in the bitterness of his heart, a mighty moralist. But we had not imagined that, of our fellow-sinners included in this category, there was one man so much a liar as to pen, in cold blood, the series of falsehoods which make up the article upon the Dutch war in yesterday's TIMES.' *(October 27, 1832.)*

'The carnage at Antwerp proceeds vigorously, to the great satisfaction, no doubt, of Lord Palmerston and his colleagues, whose policy has occasioned this horrible waste of human life.' *(December 11, 1832.)*

'It is generally believed that the answer of the King of the Netherlands to the insincere and insulting propositions of Prince Talleyrand and his lacquey, Lord Palmerston, arrived yesterday.' *(January 15, 1833.)*'

Savage though some of these comments appear, they were hardly more intemperate than the general run of newspaper controversy in the 'thirties. Winthrop Mackworth Praed, who had begun to contribute political poems to the *Morning Post* in August, 1832, became the chief leader writer at the beginning of 1833, holding that post until the Autumn of 1834. A modern biographer of Praed gives him credit for the improvement in the fortunes of the newspaper during this period. He contrasts Praed's leader-writing style with 'the uncontrolled vigour, and even ferocity, with which the early *Times* leader-writers went to work' and suggests that 'the moderate statement of editorial views to which we are now accustomed owes much, in its inception, to the graceful and gentlemanly style which Praed displayed for the first time in the *Morning Post*.'[1]

The impression left by a study of the *Morning Post* under Byrne's editorship and the slight evidence we have about his personality are too vague to provide a basis for more than a generalised portrait. To say that he was a man of stubborn convictions and unprogressive in outlook is merely to say that he was a not untypical figure of his

[1] *A Poet in Parliament*, by Derek Hudson (John Murray, 1939).

times—well meaning and honestly fearful about the political future of his country. But something more definite than this does emerge from a closer analysis of his career. It is possible to assess his journalistic stature and say that he was only a minor editor, equally devoid of professional flair and of the independence and original thinking that give character and virility to a newspaper. After thirty years of Byrne's control his too thriftily managed newspaper, which under Stuart had soared to leadership, impressed even a friendly eye as being 'only a small establishment.' Is it not because he was essentially a little man, who made no particular impression apart from editorial irascibility, that he has left hardly a trace in those abundant volumes of political and social reminiscences wherein even the mildest celebrities of the period figure in a dozen indexes?

But the mystery of the unreported murder remains. . . The world of London journalism was then a comparatively small one, and it seems hardly credible that news of the stabbing of one of its best-known editors by a masked man should not have come to the knowledge of other newspapers or of the weekly reviews, which in those days regularly printed a summary of the outstanding news. By any journalistic standard this must have been one of the most sensational news stories of the year —but not a word was printed about it anywhere. And how are we to explain the fact that no reference to the crime is made by the people who knew him and mention his name in their books—as, for instance, William Jerdan, who had worked with him on the *Morning Post* and would surely have described his violent end when he referred to his old chief in his autobiography—or by journalistic historians who wrote their books within a quarter of a century of his death? Of the latter, one does not even mention Byrne; the other has a specific reference to him and his staff but says nothing about the manner of his death.

Was Nicholas Byrne murdered? Obviously the crime would be reported to the police, and I asked Scotland Yard whether they had any records concerning him. All the likely sources were searched, but it was found impossible to trace anything on the matter. Scotland Yard pointed out, however, that the police force was not established until 1829 and early records are not complete. No reference to Byrne's death is contained in the *Morning Post* records taken over by the *Daily Telegraph* when it absorbed that paper in 1927.

Whatever the cause of his death two facts can be stated without fear of contradiction—he was not assassinated in his office and he did not die during the Winter of 1832-1833. For several months afterwards the *Morning Post* continued to carry this imprint: 'Edited and printed by Nicholas Byrne. Published by Thomas Payne, No. 335, Strand.' That imprint appeared for the last time on June 27, 1833, and the following day's issue contained this simple announcement: 'DIED—Yesterday, June 27, after an illness of many months, in his 72nd year, N. Byrne, Esq., of Lancaster-place.' A similar announcement was published in *The Times* and other newspapers. The *Morning Post* made no other reference to the death of its proprietor and editor; it did not even report his funeral, which took place two days later in the churchyard of the Savoy Chapel.

If an inquest had been held it would undoubtedly have been reported in the London newspapers, which regularly published such accounts: that no inquest was held has been confirmed by the City of London Records Office, which made a search of the City coroner's records. A suggested possible explanation is that if a full inquiry at the time of the attack failed to identify the assailant (though there is no evidence that such an inquiry was officially conducted), there would have been no point in having an inquest at the time of Byrne's death, for which purely medical reasons could then have been given.[1] Apart from the formal announcement, no reference to the death of Nicholas Byrne appeared—so far as I can trace —in any contemporary journal of any kind; and, as we have seen, the statement that he had been stabbed in his office was not published until forty years later and then conveyed the misleading impression that he died shortly after the attack. My researches have failed to bring to light any confirmation of this curiously belated account.

'The life of the proprietor was twice attempted,' according to the writer in the centenary number of the *Morning Post*. The violent assault by the mob on the small *Morning Post* office during the Queen Caroline agitation in 1820 could have resulted in the death of Nicholas Byrne (though we have no record that he was present that night), and it is a reasonable hypothesis that the writer had this in mind as the occasion of the first attempt on his life; or was it a more directly personal attack which, like the stabbing, remarkably escaped publicity at the time? It is not one of the least peculiar circumstances of this strange affair that Julia C. Byrne, who describes the mob attack on the *Morning Post* offices, makes no reference to the more dramatic fact of the stabbing of her father-in-law by a masked assailant. If the motive for the attack on his life was political, there does not seem to be any reason for suppressing the story in a book that was written sixty years after the event. Or was the secret so closely guarded that William Pitt Byrne, who did not marry until nine years after his father's death, never revealed it to his wife? Or, knowing the truth about the affair, did she purposely avoid any reference to the story belatedly published in 1872?

We must assume, incredible though it appears to anyone living in our own age of instantaneous publicity, that

[1] National registration of death and the cause of death had not yet been made compulsory. No certificate is therefore available for reference.

the attack did take place and that Byrne did pursue his assailant to the street—a fact which suggests that the immediate effect of his injuries was not severe—and that no one outside the office knew anything about it. We must further assume that knowledge of the attack was limited to one or two trusted members of his staff, that Byrne was still sufficiently master of himself to command them at once to keep silent about the affair, and that no report on the attempt on his life was made to the police. That discreet silence—the reasons for which are unlikely ever to become known—miraculously lasted for forty years, and but for the brief reference in the centenary issue of the *Morning Post* the secret would probably never have been disclosed.

The story calls for a brief postscript by way of comment on the omission of the *Morning Post* to publish a biography of its proprietor after his death. This had not necessarily anything to do with the murderous attack made on him; the memoir could have been confined to an account of his career. A simpler explanation suggests itself. Nicholas Byrne probably took the austere view that no reference to the proprietor or the editor should be made in the editorial columns of his journal—a journalistic tradition that is not yet completely extinct—and carried this principle to the extreme point of instructing his staff, as he must surely have done, not to print any biography of him or to make any reference to his passing apart from the formal death notice (which did not contain, it will have been noted, any mention of his connection with the paper). Over sixty years later a more famous editor-owner was to act on this principle, though not quite so thoroughly as Byrne. Charles A. Dana, editor of the *New York Sun*, left instructions that the paper was to print only two lines about his death. The announcement, exactly this length, duly appeared after his death in 1897. It was on the editorial page and stated quite simply:

'Charles Anderson Dana, editor of the *Sun*, died yesterday afternoon.' When Thomas Barnes, editor of *The Times* from 1817 to 1841, died the paper contained no reference beyond this brief announcement in the 'Deaths' column: 'On the 7th inst., at his house in Soho-Square, Thomas Barnes, Esq., in the 56th year of his age.' When, however, John Walter II, the chief proprietor, died in 1847, Delane published a memoir of him extending to three and a half columns.

The Three Trials of
William Hone

*

WILLIAM Hone would now be remembered (rather vaguely) only as the editor of the *Every-day Book,* a once-popular miscellany, if the authorities had not made the blunder of prosecuting him for publishing three irreverent parodies. Though he edited also a small periodical, he would have left hardly a trace in the history of journalism but for the accident of the three trials that compelled him to stand forth as a sturdy champion of free expression. To the Attorney-General he was a person of no consequence, and it was only necessary to follow the usual routine to ensure conviction; but both he and the famous judge who presided at the second and third trials were defied by this seemingly commonplace man who was said never to have been in a court before. Who could have imagined that this struggling bookseller, far from being terrified by the formidable machine of prosecution that had already claimed so many victims, would so humiliate the Government that it halted its campaign against the Press for months until it had regained its confidence to strike? Small wonder that this David-and-Goliath spectacle made Hone a popular hero and that reports of the trials were eagerly bought.

It was the little men, like Richard Carlile (who suffered years of imprisonment) and William Hone, booksellers and editors and authors of no special talent but who possessed invincible courage—it was these "minor" figures who were responsible for the final defeat of the forces of oppression. Even Cobbett, who struck mighty blows for the liberty of the Press, was not so brave as

these little men when it came to the test; once, under
Government pressure, he prepared a 'farewell article'
(unpublished) in which he undertook never to write again
for a newspaper, and on another occasion he fled to
America to escape prosecution. Neither Carlile nor Hone
would have yielded to pressure or run away rather than
face their persecutors.

Hone was born in 1780, and the story of his life up to
the time of the trials in 1817 followed a dreary pattern
of ups and downs that seemed to stamp him as one of
life's inevitable failures. After working for some years—
from the early age of ten—in lawyers' offices, he married
at twenty and set up in business as a bookseller (later a
printseller) in Lambeth Walk, which in those days was
surrounded by gardens. His mother-in-law advanced him
£100 capital, and it was to her that he turned—and
apparently never in vain—at the recurring economic
crises that disagreeably punctuated his career for many
years to come.

About 1806 he made the acquaintance of John Bone, a
Dutchman who had found sanctuary in England after
escaping from the Bastille, and they soon became not
only friends but business associates. They were both
attracted by the conception of savings banks and their
advantages alike to the individual and the country: an
idea that fulfilled its promise in firm and competent
hands later but came to grief when the two idealists
started a well-meaning but amateurish venture. They set
up in Albion Place, Blackfriars, an institution that com
bined the features of a savings bank, insurance office and
employment registry, and they styled it 'Tranquillity,'
which would have been an odd and meaningless name
in any circumstances but in the event was to prove an
unhappy choice. Men of substance, including Sir William Stirling, had sufficient faith in Hone and his partner
to act as trustees. Unfortunately the bank quickly failed,
and the funds available being insufficient to cover ex-

penses the debtors seized Hone's furniture in distraint.
Next the two men conducted a bookshop, but this venture was also unsuccessful. In 1811 the booksellers appointed Hone trade auctioneer and he had a counting-
house in Ivy Lane, but the sales were not frequent
enough to supply the needs of his wife and seven children. Most of his ventures failed because he lacked ade-
quate capital and because he took more interest in public
affairs than in his business.

He had begun to write occasionally and had contributions accepted by the *Critical Review* and the *British
Lady's Magazine,* and in 1815 (at which time he had a
small shop at 55, Fleet Street, where he was robbed three
times) he was publisher of the *Traveller* newspaper, for
which he wrote a defence of Elizabeth Fenning. He also
issued a number of pamphlets, probably not all of which
were written by himself; thirteen appeared in 1815-1816.
Early in 1817—the year in which he was to emerge from
obscurity to become a national figure—he started the
Reformist's Register (a 16-page octavo weekly sold at
twopence), and about the same time he was very active in
writing satires. His little periodical struggled on for three
quarters of a year—from February 1 to October 25—and
had to be discontinued because of the cares of 'a little
business and a large family.' Among his satires were three
parodies, not in good taste but sharply pointed and effective—*The Late John Wilkes's Catechism of a Ministerial
Member, The Political Litany* and *The Sinecurist's Creed,
or Belief.* The Attorney-General laid three informa-
tions against William Hone for 'printing and publishing certain impious, profane and scandalous libels'—
the real but unstated reason for the prosecution was that
he attacked the Government in these satires—and because
he could not find £1,000 bail he was committed to prison
on May 3 and remained there two months, when he was

released on his own recognisances.[1] He was tried in the following December.

To defend himself against a public prosecution for libel, in the harshly intolerant atmosphere of the post-Waterloo days, was an ordeal even for the stoutest hearted of men; to defend himself successfully in three cases, one after the other, might well have seemed a hopeless prospect to Hone. Whatever his private thoughts may have been, he never showed any want of confidence or spirit in court. The Attorney-General had no doubt that he would be able to crush this insignificant but obnoxious bookseller, but to his dismay—and that of the two judges concerned—Hone was found to be possessed of a dogged courage and resource in argument that enabled him to dominate the court throughout the proceedings.

The first case, concerning the mock catechism, was heard before Mr. Justice Abbott and a special jury on December 18. The offending parody began (and this extract typifies the rest):

Question. 'What is your name?
Answer. 'Lick Spittle.
Q. 'Who gave you this name?
A. 'My Sureties to the Ministry, in my Political Change, wherein I was made a Member of the Majority, the Child of Corruption, and a Locust to devour the good Things of this Kingdom.'

In his long speech in his own defence, Hone mainly relied on the argument that he was to employ in the two succeeding trials—that parodies were as old as the inven-

---

[1] He continued to write while in prison, telling his readers: 'I wrote my last *Register* at home in the midst of my family. Since then the Reign of Terror has commenced, and I now write from prison.'

tion of printing and that he had never heard of a prosecution for a parody, either religious or any other. He
cited in particular a parody entitled *The Chaldee Manuscript* which had been published in *Blackwood's Magazine* several months after his arrest, and he observed that
William Blackwood was respected by a great number of
persons. The judge said he could not think their respect
could be increased by such a publication; he must express
his disapprobation of it, and at the same time observe
that the defendant, by citing it, was only defending one
offence by another. Hone, however, was intent on doing
this very thing, and neither Mr. Justice Abbott nor the
judge at the second and third trials—Lord Chief Justice
Ellenborough—succeeded in restraining him. He proceeded to quote parodies written by Luther, Erasmus,
Bishop Latimer and a Dean of Canterbury. Again the
judge commented that one instance of profaneness could
not excuse another. Hone agreed, but said that if this
mode of writing had been practised by dignitaries of the
Church and by men high in the State, he conceived that
that circumstance might be some excuse for his having
been the publisher of the trifle now charged as libellous.
He had never had any idea of ridiculing religion, and as
soon as he became aware that the publication had given
offence to some persons whose opinion he respected he
stopped the sale.

Hone continued to quote parodies that had appeared
before his own and towards the end of his speech he
produced a trump card—a parody entitled *The New
Morality: or, The Installation of the High Priest*, written
for the *Anti-Jacobin* by Canning, 'who ought, at this
moment, to be standing in my place, but who has been
raised to the rank of Cabinet Minister and is one of those
very men who are now persecuting me.' In his summing-
up the judge said he was convinced that the production
was highly scandalous and irreligious and therefore libellous. The jury, after only a quarter of an hour's retire-

ment, found Hone not guilty. 'The loudest acclamations were instantly heard in all parts of the Court; *Long live the honest Jury*, and *an honest Jury for ever*, were exclaimed by many voices: the waving of hats, handkerchiefs, and applause continued for several minutes.'[1]

The second trial, for publishing *The Political Litany*, was heard before Lord Ellenborough and a special jury the next day and aroused even greater interest. When the doors were opened 'not one-twentieth part of the multitude could find standing accommodation.' After the Attorney-General had referred to the satire as a 'dangerous, impious and profane publication,' the clerk read the parody to the Court. A brief extract will indicate the flavour of the whole:

'From an unnational debt; from unmerited pensions and sinecure places; from an extravagant civil list; and from utter starvation, *Good Prince, deliver us.* From the blind imbecility of ministers; from the pride and vainglory of warlike establishments in time of peace, *Good Prince, deliver us.*'

When Hone, in his speech for the defence, urged that without the production of former parodies it was impossible for the jury to come to a sound decision upon the allegations against him, Lord Ellenborough said that such evidence would be judicially inadmissible. With any ordinary defendant that would have been the end of it, but Hone refused to be silenced. He asked the judge whether he really meant to send him to prison without a trial. Lord Ellenborough said that while he could state what he knew to be of service to him, nothing such as he had described could be given in evidence—but despite this Hone followed the same line of defence as at the first trial. When he was protesting against the refusal to

[1] *The First Trial of William Hone.* (Sold in pamphlet form at a shilling. My copy is the 20th edition.)

provide him with a copy of the information and cited a case at Chester as a gross example of this 'tyrannical proceeding,' the judge told him that he was only wasting time. Hone retorted:

'Wasting time, my Lord! I feel the grievance of which I complain; I am to be tried, not you! When I shall have been consigned to a dungeon, your Lordship will sit as coolly on that seat as ever; you will not feel the punishment; I feel the grievance, and I remonstrate against it. I am the injured man. I am upon my trial by those *gentlemen*, my jury.'

When he complained that a newspaper had libelled him and the judge demanded what that had to do with him or the jury Hone interrupted him passionately: 'My Lord! my Lord! it is *I* who am upon my trial, *not your Lordship*. I have to defend myself, not your Lordship.' He proceeded to quote from various parodies of religious texts, and was warned by Lord Ellenborough that under pretence of defending himself from one crime he was not to commit another; but again he ignored this ruling. Coming to his own parody, he said that he was prepared to go through every supplication to show that it was true, not libellous, but a juryman told him that it was not necessary to read any further: 'we are satisfied.' In his charge to the jury the judge pronounced Hone's parody to be a most impious and profane libel, and believing that they were Christians he had not any doubt they would be of the same opinion. 'His Lordship, who appeared much oppressed with indisposition during the latter part of the trial, delivered this charge in so faint a tone, that it was scarcely audible, beyond the Bench.'[1] The jury retired and after an hour and three quarters returned with a verdict of not guilty. There were again demonstrations of approval in court.

[1] *The Second Trial of William Hone.*

The third trial—in respect of *The Sinecurist's Creed*—was proceeded with the next day. It was the defendant who was now observed to be indisposed, and the Attorney-General said that Mr. Hone appeared to be very unwell and it had just been suggested that a delay in the proceedings might be necessary, 'in consideration of his probable inadequacy to enter upon his defence with the full command of those energies which he possesses to a very considerable degree.' Hone expressed thanks for the offer of indulgence and said he was merely exhausted from the effort of the day before: in a little time he hoped to be so recovered as to be able to enter upon his defence.[1]

The Attorney-General's speech was followed as usual by the reading of the parody—a tasteless satire not worth sampling. It was remarked that Hone 'seemed weak, and not collected in his mind.' The judge asked him whether he desired to have the trial postponed. Immediately Hone seemed to recover his strength and his self-possession and firmly declined to make any such request, and then addressed Lord Ellenborough with calculated aggressiveness.

'I am very glad to see your Lordship here today, because I feel that I sustained an injury from your Lordship yesterday. . . If the proceedings of a solemn trial, like that of yesterday, are to be interrupted—and I say that because I think your Lordship gave——

Lord Ellenborough: 'I cannot hear any observations in that way now, on what passed yesterday. You may make common and ordinary observations, but I cannot sit here to be attacked.'

---

[1] It is stated at the end of *The Third Trial of William Hone* that on the first day he spoke for nearly six hours, on the second day for nearly seven hours and on the third day for upwards of eight hours.

A few minutes later, when he was reading a comment on a statute concerning a judge's powers, Lord Ellenborough interrupted him with an observation on the statute. Hone, 'earnestly and slowly,' protested with shrewd rhetorical effect.

'My Lord, I think it necessary to make a stand here. I cannot say what your Lordship may consider to be a necessary interruption, but your Lordship interrupted me a great many times yesterday, and then said you would interrupt me no more. Gentlemen, it is you who are trying me today. His Lordship is no judge of me. You are *my* judges, and *you only* are my judges. His Lordship sits there to receive your verdict. He does not even sit there to regulate the trial—for *the law* has already regulated it. He sits there only as the administrator of the law.'

Later Hone said it had been suggested that he should engage counsel to defend him, but some objections were urged against all whose names were mentioned.

'The question I put, upon such recommendation to counsel being made, was, has he *courage*? Will he be able to stand up against my Lord Ellenborough? Will he withstand the browbeating of my Lord Ellenborough?'

The Attorney-General: 'I cannot sit here quietly and hear such language directed to the court. I submit, my Lord, whether it be right.

Lord Ellenborough: 'Perhaps, Mr. Attorney, you might have interposed your objection sooner; but you have heard the sort of attack which was made upon me. I think the best course will be to let the whole thing blow over us!'

Presently Hone introduced into his speech a chapter of autobiography, describing his various misfortunes and (with gross exaggeration, as events proved) declaring that

he had not a friend in the world. The appeal to the jury
was frankly emotional. 'Just as I was getting my head
above water, this storm assailed me, and plunged me
deeper than ever. . . I have ever been independent in
mind, and hence I am a destitute man. I have never
written or printed what I did not think right and true;
and in my most humble station have always acted for
the public good, according to my conception, without
regard to what other men did, however exalted their
rank.' Then, with a swift change of mood, he told the
jury that his parody was written for a political purpose—
to produce a laugh against the Ministers. 'He had laughed
at them, and, ha! ha! ha! he laughed at them now, and he
would laugh at them, as long as they were laughing-
stocks. Were there any poor witless men less ridiculous
than these ministers, his persecutors; one of whom himself was a parodist, winking at, instigating, aiding and
abetting this persecution. George Canning was a parodist,
with William Hone and Martin Luther.' Whereupon—
the report tells us—there was applause.

In his charge to the jury Lord Ellenborough begged
them were not prohibited and punished, the country was
them to recollect that if such publications as that before
liable to be deluged by irreligion and impiety, which had
so lately produced such melancholy results in another
nation. The jury quickly reached a verdict. After twenty
minutes' retirement they pronounced Hone not guilty—
and the crowded court loudly expressed approval.

The trials had a remarkable sequel. Far from Hone
being without friends, he had many influential people on
his side and thousands of well-wishers all over the country. A public meeting was held at the City of London
Tavern ten days later for the purpose of starting a fund.
Robert Waithman was in the chair, and speeches were
made by Sir Francis Burdett, Lord Cochrane, James
Perry (editor of the *Morning Chronicle*) and others. Several country newspapers, 'considering that the Liberty of

the Public Press has been essentially promoted by Mr. Hone's exertions,' opened books for subscriptions at their offices. Altogether £3,000 was raised and Hone was enabled to move to a large shop at 45, Ludgate Hill; but only one third of the sum came to him, for £1,000 went in expenses and another £1,000 was stolen by a collector.[1]

Lord Ellenborough, who had presided at the trial of James Perry for a libel on the King and at the two trials of the Hunt brothers and had the reputation of being a terror to juries (not confirmed by his bearing at the Hone trials), was so mortified at 'the disgraceful events which have occurred at the Guildhall within the last three or four days' that he sent in his resignation. He died the following year. Though he had been in ill health for several years, a widely held view was that he died of a broken heart.

Hone lived for a quarter of a century after the trials, and for most of that time he was busily engaged in writing and publishing, including the production of six-penny reprints known as 'Hone's Editions.' *The Every-day Book*, begun in 1826, sold badly at first and led to his being imprisoned for debt: he finished the writing of the work in the King's Bench. He achieved most success with political squibs, notably *The Political House that Jack Built* (written in 1819 and illustrated by George Cruikshank), which went into fifty-four editions. In *A Slap at Slop* he burlesqued the *New Times* and ridiculed its editor, Dr. John Stoddart (who started his paper after being dismissed from the editorship of *The Times*). In its blasting manner the *Quarterly Review* stigmatised Hone as 'a wretch as contemptible as he is wicked,' but there were many of his contemporaries who saw in him one who, despite crudities of taste and expression, was as honest as he was courageous. Charles Lamb was among his friends, and Hone dedicated his *Every-day Book* to

[1] *William Hone: His Life and Times*, by F. W. Hackwood (Fisher Unwin, 1912).

him. Lamb wrote these pleasant lines in the first of the verses that he addressed *To the Editor of the Every-day Book:*

'I like you, and your book, ingenious Hone!
In whose capacious, all-embracing leaves
The very marrow of tradition's shown;
And all that history—much that fiction—weaves.'

Hone became devout in later years, and by invitation preached from time to time at the Weigh House Chapel in Eastcheap. In 1837, when he was sub-editor of the *Patriot*, he had an attack of paralysis. He died five years later, and among those who attended the funeral were Charles Dickens and Cruikshank.

'Bright, Broken Maginn'

•

To contemporary moralists the career of William Maginn must have appeared as an Awful Warning; to the more indulgent eyes of posterity it has a kind of disreputable charm and can at times inspire a reluctantly affectionate interest; and to Thackeray, Lockhart and other friends who remained faithful to the end, nothing could obscure the shining fact that Maginn was the most lovable as well as the wittiest of human beings.

The adventure began so well. In that marvellous springtime at Cork, when the phenomenal boy, son of a fine classical scholar, was delighting his father with his extraordinary gifts, it must have appeared to all who knew him that he was destined for great things.

If Maginn did not fulfil the splendid promise of his youth it was not because the flame of his genius (the word is not excessive) flickered out: almost to the end he continued to impress even the most sophisticated judges with his brilliance and his amazing versatility. In a book purporting to describe the proceedings of a 'Deipnosophist Club' (with Maginn as its president), his friend Edward Vaughan Kenealy gives this playfully heightened picture of the many rôles he played: "Theologian, Historian, Poet, Metaphysician, Mathematician, Philosopher, Phrenologist, Stenographist, Fencer, Boxer, Orator, Dramatist, Reviewer, Sonnetteer, Joker, Punster, Doctor of Laws, Hoaxer, Political Economist, Newspaper Editor, Wit, Duellist, Pedestrian, Linguist, Arithmetician, Scholar, O'Doherty, Pamphleteer, Translator, Epigrammatist, Antiquarian, Conversationalist, Novelist and true Tory to the backbone.'[1] This catalogue sticks close to the facts

[1] *Brallaghan, or the Deipnosophists,* by E. V. Kenealy (1845). Kenealy was later to become widely known as chief counsel for the claimant in the prolonged Tichborne trial.

of Maginn's career: the apparently obscure O'Doherty is a reference to his favourite pen name.

There were to be the memorable days when he revealed the rapier flash of his wit in *Blackwood's Magazine,* when he was joint editor of the *Standard* and when later his contributions to *Fraser's Magazine* were the talk of the town; there were to be shabby interludes of less reputable journalism to which he was driven by drink and debts; and there were to be the years of miserable anti-climax ending in the debtors' prison and the lonely death at Walton-on-Thames of 'bright, broken Maginn'— to quote from the epitaph written by J. G. Lockhart. But if the promise of his youth was not fulfilled, if he had at times prostituted his pen and at other times used it with malicious irresponsibility, he did make a prodigious impression for some years on the literary and journalistic scene, as a writer of all the talents and as a brilliant personality and gentle, warm-hearted man who, as one of his closest friends testified, retained his serenity almost to the dreadful last days.

William Maginn was born on July 10, 1794,[1] at Cork, where his father conducted a private school for boys. His aptitude for learning, especially in the field of classical studies, was so remarkable that he entered Trinity College, Dublin, at the age of eleven.[2] On his return to Cork, after graduation, he became a classical teacher in his father's school, and he carried on after the latter died in 1813. He had a special talent for languages and was

---

[1] In 1793 according to the *Dictionary of National Biography,* but the date is given as 1794 by *Fraser's Magazine* and the *Dublin University Magazine,* and on the tombstone in Walton-on-Thames churchyard.

[2] The matriculation records of Trinity College reveal that he was entered on January 6, 1806, and that his age was given as eleven —which confirms that he was born in 1794. The commencement lists show that the degree of B.A. was conferred on July 9, 1811— the day before his seventeenth birthday.

credited with the ability to speak and write fluently French, German, Italian, Spanish, Portuguese and modern Greek, besides having a knowledge of Hebrew (for which he gained a prize), Sanskrit and Syriac before he was twenty-five; and subsequently he mastered the Swedish, Russian and Basque languages. Irish he had known since he was a child, and later he was to make a comparative study of two other Celtic languages—Welsh and Gaelic. His memory was prodigious, 'the strongest in the world,' declared Edward Kenealy: it was 'a rich storehouse of all learning, so that he might with propriety be called, like the sublime Longinus, "the living library." And yet, like Scott, no eye ever saw him reading. He seemed a perfectly idle man, and knowledge to come to him by intuition.'

Trinity College awarded Maginn the degrees of LL.B. and LL.D. in 1819. It was about this time that he began his journalistic writing, contributing to William Jerdan's *Literary Gazette* and to *Blackwood's Magazine* (signing himself R. T. Scott). William Blackwood ('Ebony') was very curious as to the identity of his brilliant contributor but did not make his acquaintance until a year or so later, when Maginn visited Edinburgh to introduce himself. He became a member of the remarkable *Blackwood's Magazine* team that also included John Gibson Lockhart, Professor John Wilson (Christopher North) and James Hogg, writing regularly for the magazine under the new and very Irish pseudonym of Morgan O'Doherty. He invented, and contributed to, the famous 'Noctes Ambrosianae' feature.

There is much about Maginn's connection with *Maga* in *William Blackwood and Sons* (1897), the history of the firm written by Mrs. Oliphant—with a prefatory expression of Victorian disapproval to explain why he is relegated to a chapter not immediately following those devoted to Lockhart and Wilson. 'Such a man cannot have justice from the world, scarcely even pity. It is almost immoral to be sorry for him, or to remember that once he was young and an emblem of all that was joyous, delightful, and gay.' We find Lockhart, in one of his numerous undated letters, urging Blackwood to get Maginn to do more writing for his magazine. 'Do persuade him to give you more of his mind, and his beautiful scholarship.' Blackwood required no urging to do this. He had an immense admiration for the writing of Maginn, and not even the fact that very early in their association he had involved the magazine in a libel action (with £100 in damages to add to heavy costs) damped his enthusiasm for this gifted new contributor. Apparently Maginn refused payment for his articles except in kind (as, for instance, when he asked for 'the latest and best Syriac, Chaldee, and Samaritan grammars') until he decided to give up teaching and become a professional writer.

Once Maginn saved *Blackwood's* from a libel action that would have been most embarrassing to the magazine: the prospect of it reduced Wilson to hysteria, the reason being that Christopher North ('monarch of magazinists,' as *Maga* once called him) was menaced with exposure as a guest who had promptly and meanly repaid Wordsworth, recently his host, with a sneering reference to his work. In one of the 'Noctes' (September, 1825) Wilson had, in the first place, made a vulgar attack on Richard Martin, an Irish M.P. who had been successful in getting the House of Commons to pass an Act for the prevention of (and punishment for) cruelty to animals. When Martin threatened to bring an action and demanded the writer's name, Wilson had a moral collapse because in the same dialogue he had said: 'Wordsworth often writes like an idiot. . . Wordsworth is, in all things, the reverse of Milton—a good man, and a bad poet. . . I confess that the "Excursion" is the worst poem of any character in the language. . . And then how ludicrously he overrates his own poems. This we all do; but Wordsworth's pride is like that of a straw-crowned king of

Bedlam.' Yet a few weeks before he had stayed with
Wordsworth at Rydal Mount. . . In a letter to Blackwood
he wrote:

'On reading your enclosures I was seized with a
trembling and shivering fit, and was deadly sick for some
hours. . . To own that article is for a thousand reasons
impossible. It would involve me in lies abhorrent to my
nature. I would rather die this evening. . . This avowal
would be fatal to my character, my peace, to existence.
Say nothing to me that could add to my present misery. . .
Were I to go to London it would be to throw myself into
the Thames.'

'The Professor really seems to act on such occasions as
if he were mad,' wrote Lockhart to Blackwood, and Mrs.
Oliphant plausibly suggests that the hand of Lockhart
was discernible in an apologetic letter headed 'Mid-
summer Madness and Mr. Martin' which appeared in
the next issue of the magazine. To Blackwood's relief
Maginn agreed to approach Martin—'we Irish know how
to talk to each other'—and try to settle the matter
amicably, and the fact that the apology included an
account of the work of 'that most humane and generous
individual' helped him in his delicate mission. He per-
suaded Martin to have dinner with him. 'He was very
angry at first, but I outtalked him. I shall make you
laugh, I think, when I see you at our conversation; but it
would be no good to detail it.' And the letter ended, very
characteristically: 'I think I did a good job for you. As I
cannot offer to give people champagne at my own
expense, I charge you the bill, which, like Falstaff's, is
rather heavier in the drinking than in the eating. It
amounts in all to £3, 7s., with which I debit you.' Blackwood must have been delighted to settle an ugly business
at such a trifling cost.

Maginn had then been in London for two years. In

1823, at the age of twenty-nine, he had handed over the school at Cork to his brother John, got married (to the daughter of an Irish rector) and gone to live in London in order to devote himself entirely to writing. He quickly gained a footing there, helped by his association with *Blackwood's* and the *Literary Gazette*. John Murray took an interest in him and wanted to commission him to write a life of Byron, but found that Maginn was not attracted by the subject. When in 1826 he started the *Representative*—a daily paper that lived only six months and involved him in a heavy loss—the publisher sent Maginn to Paris as foreign correspondent at £500 a year. He was not a success—it was said that he proved better at borrowing money than writing articles—and Murray recalled him to serve on the editorial staff at £700 a year. It was while he was working on the *Representative* that the weakness which was to be mainly responsible for the wrecking of his career became manifest—his intemperance. With his excessive liking for drink went an extravagance and fecklessness that had already got him into debt and that would plunge him into financial straits from time to time right up to the end of his life.[1]

In addition to regular contributions to *Blackwood's* and the *Literary Gazette* he was now writing articles for the *Quarterly Review*, which was edited by Lockhart. He was also doing occasional work for Theodore Hook's *John Bull*, a not very reputable weekly; and through Hook's introduction he became closely associated a year or two later with Charles M. Westmacott, a notorious journalist who had bought the *Age* and was using it as an instrument for extracting blackmail[2]. By contrast with

[1] When one of Maginn's friends remarked on the excellent port which he gave to his guests and asked whether it was not very expensive, he received the casual reply: 'I don't know. I believe they do put something down in a book.' (Quoted in *L.E.L.: A Mystery of the 'Thirties*, by D. E. Enfield—Hogarth Press, 1928.)

[2] An outline of Westmacott's unsavoury career is given in Mr Michael Sadleir's *Bulwer and His Wife* (Constable, 1931).

these questionable activities Maginn was about this time (1828) chosen as joint editor of a new evening paper, the *Standard*—and the previous year his clever satirical novel, *Whitehall, or the Days of George IV*, had appeared. If his way of life had allowed him to devote time to writing of permanent value, instead of being dominated by his ever-present need to write something that he could immediately turn into cash, he might well have gained a name that would now be known to the general reader and not merely to the student of the period. The nagging pressure of financial troubles condemned him to waste his genius on ephemeral writing—some of it, as already noted, of a degrading type.

Maginn had many friends of influence in the literary and journalistic world. Several have been mentioned: another was Thomas Barnes, editor of *The Times*, whom he had got to know soon after arriving in London. According to *The History of 'The Times,'* the destructive reviews of Bulwer Lytton's novels that appeared in that journal may have been contributed by Maginn. The official history also reveals that he was probably the originator of the nickname 'The Blunderer,' first used in a paragraph that appeared in the *Morning Herald* of February 15, signed 'P.P.P.' (initials that William Jerdan's autobiography assigns to Maginn). In this paragraph *The Times* is described as 'The Great Earwigger of the Nation, otherwise the Leading Journal of Europe, otherwise The Awful Monosyllable, otherwise the Thunderer—but more commonly called "The Blunderer".'

It was not only in the columns of *The Times* that he attacked Bulwer Lytton. This fashionable novelist of the time (who incidentally has an honourable place in the history of the British Press as one of its leading champions in the campaign to remove the 'taxes on knowledge') was the target of venomous attacks by Maginn in the pages of

...nding of this famous ...er in Maginn's

ERRATUM

Page 75, line 22:
for "The Blunderer" read "The Thunderer."

career, the period when he was writing at his most brilliant, when he was a potent name in the field of literary criticism and when—on the surface—everything seemed to be going well for him. The full title of the new periodical was *Fraser's Magazine for Town and Country,* and it was named after Hugh Fraser, a well-known man about town who was associated with Maginn in starting it, and not (as generally assumed) after James Fraser, its publisher.

Maginn was editor in all but name in the early days and wrote a large part of the contents: it was his wit and inventiveness that gave this new literary magazine its original quality, made it a serious rival of *Blackwood's* and attracted such distinguished contributors as Carlyle, Thackeray and Lockhart. Thackeray took a great liking to Maginn—and helped him financially, lending him £500 (the verb was probably a euphemism). Two of the many references to him in Thackeray's diary and letters[1] may be quoted:

May 1, 1832: 'Dr. Maginn called and took me to the *Standard* shewing me the mysteries of printing and writing leading articles. With him all day till 4.'

May 12, 1832: 'Dined at Montague Place and was introduced to Fraser of F's Magazine—thought him neither clever or good very different to hearty witty Maginn, who is a very loveable man I think.'

No feature of *Fraser's Magazine* was more talked about than Maginn's 'Gallery of Illustrious Characters' (later produced in volume form and still highly readable), graced with delightful pencil drawings by Daniel Maclise. In the writing of these swift and acute impressions of leading authors of the day Maginn was at his most

[1] *The Letters and Private Papers of William Makepeace Thackeray,* collected and edited by Gordon N. Ray (Harvard University Press, 1946).

humorous and felicitous, and he became generally recognised as one of the foremost journalists and critics of the age. Another series that Maginn contributed was called the 'Fraser Papers'—'written on subjects generally of a temporary nature, and every one of them hastily struck off in Fraser's back parlour, over such supplies of liquor as would totally incapacitate all other men from work.'[1]

What kind of impression did Maginn make on his friends at the height of his fame? This vivid portrait from the pen of Edward Kenealy—part of an outline of Maginn's career that appeared after his death[1]—would seem over-generous but for the warmth of the tributes to his kindliness and charm from so many of his literary friends.

'No formal looking personage, in customary suit of solemn black, stood before me—but a slight, boyish, careless figure, with a blue eye, the mildest ever seen—hair, not exactly white, but of a sunned snow colour—an easy, familiar smile—and a countenance, that you would be more inclined to laugh with, than feel terror from. He bounded across the room, with a most unscholar-like eagerness, and warmly welcomed the visitor, asking him a thousand questions, and putting him at his ease in a moment. . . Then was to be seen the kindness and gentleness of heart which tinged every word and gesture with sweetness, suavity and mildness, so strongly the reverse of what was to be expected from the most galling satirist of the day.'

But there was a dark side to the nature of this man who could appear so gentle and kindly to his friends. There were moments when his talent for sarcasm degenerated into sheer malice, when he seemed to be completely deficient in scruple and simple human feeling. Never was this recklessness more crudely displayed than

[1] *Dublin University Magazine,* January, 1844.

in the review which he wrote in 1836 of the Hon. Grantley Berkeley's novel *Berkeley Castle*. The three brief extracts that follow will probably appear to justify the description of the review subsequently given in court as one of 'cold-blooded, deliberate malignity.'

'We are far from being desirous to insult, as the paltry author of this book itself, the character of woman; but when matters are recorded in solemn judgments, there can be no indelicacy in stating that Mr. Grantley Berkeley's mother lived with Mr. Grantley Berkeley's father as his mistress, and that she had at least one child before she could induce the old and very stupid lord to marry her. All this is set down in the Journals of the House of Lords. Why then, under such circumstances, bore us with long panegyrics upon the purity, antiquity, and nobility of the Berkeley blood?'

'But it is idle to break such a cockroach upon the wheel. In every thing the novel is stupid, ignorant, vulgar, and contemptible.'

'It must lead to the conclusion that the man who formed such a conception would be ready to. . . lie and pimp, under any circumstances, with as much alacrity as the cherished model of his brain.'

Berkeley, who had already gained ill-repute as a rake and a bully, decided to have his revenge in the traditional manner of his kind. Accompanied by his brother, he called upon James Fraser and demanded the name and address of the author of the review. Fraser replied that it was not his custom to reveal the names of contributors. After a further refusal and a warning to Fraser of the consequences, Berkeley made a violent assault upon him, for which he and his brother were later prosecuted. What happened was thirty years later described with insensitive candour by Berkeley himself:

'I at once with my fist knocked him down on his desk whence on his recovering he snatched at some weapon close behind him. I never knew what it was, but, seizing him by the collar, hurled him into the middle of his shop; where, on his refusing to rise, and on my brother handing me a racing-whip he had brought for my use, I gave him a severe flogging, which concluded in the gutter of the street, up which he presently fled, crying loudly for help. . . As I released Mr. Fraser, the crowd quickly encircled me. There were loud demands for a policeman.'[1]

Though Berkeley had received extreme provocation, there could be no defence for this attack by a big and powerfully built man on a small, frail person who was not, in any case, the real object of his wrath. The case against the brothers was heard in the Exchequer Court. Fraser was awarded £100 damages, and in a cross-action for libel a verdict was entered by consent for the plaintiff with damages of 40s., each party paying his own costs. The January, 1837 issue of *Fraser's* contained a full report of the case, followed by an attempted justification by Maginn. On hearing of the assault he had left his card at Grantley Berkeley's house. A meeting was quickly arranged to take place in a field just off the Harrow Road —then a quiet spot a few miles out of town. The duel was a serio-comic affair: probably the fiasco was deliberately intended by both men. Berkeley, reputedly a first-class shot, would be especially anxious not to get on the wrong side of the law at a time when he was already a notorious figure; Maginn was concerned only to make a gesture, with the minimum of risk and discomfort to himself. Berkeley's first shot hit the pistol case on the ground and (he says) part of the hinge went into his opponent's boot. When Maginn fired his shot struck the ground close to his foot. Both men missed at the

[1] *My Life and Recollections,* by the Hon. Grantley Berkeley (1865).

second attempt and Maginn's third shot also went wide. There is a clash of evidence about Berkeley's third shot: only he appeared to get the impression that it drew blood. When Maginn was asked whether he wished the duel to continue he retorted, 'Blaze away, by God! a barrel of powder!' but this exclamation must have seemed merely rhetorical to his second (Hugh Fraser), who insisted that the duel be broken off.

In his reminiscences Berkeley refers to another unpleasant episode in Maginn's career—his association with L.E.L. (Letitia Elizabeth Landon, 1802-1838). This association was almost certainly innocent on her part, but it was to have ruinous consequences for her personal reputation and her happiness. L.E.L., a brave but pathetic figure, had with small talent but great industry supported her family by her literary earnings since the age of eighteen. She owed her early success to the influence of William Jerdan, a friend of the family, to whose *Literary Gazette* she contributed poems and reviews. Her gift for sentimental versifying was very much to the taste of the age, and she became the most popular contributor to the agreeably produced annuals—keepsakes, albums and scrapbooks—which had an immense sale in those days.

Maginn, as mentioned earlier, was also writing for the *Literary Gazette* in the eighteen-twenties. L.E.L. was flattered by the friendly interest of this brilliant, humorous man, who generously advised her and even (some years later) wrote some of the poems that appeared under her signature in an annual that she edited (Fisher's *Drawing-Room Scrap Book*)—an easy feat for a writer with a fluent gift for parody. There does not appear to have been anything more than a flirtation on her part, but sufficient is known of Maginn's fondness for girls to confirm the belief that he aimed at her seduction. She was romantic in the respectable, popular-fictional sense of that much-worn word, and she was human enough to enjoy the admiration of the clever writers with whom she came in contact through her work. This naive friendliness seemed to be indiscreet to some of her friends, especially in an age when the spectacle of a not unpersonable young female earning a considerable income as a writer for magazines and annuals and moving about freely in the literary world would be viewed with a mixture of envy and alarm.

L.E.L. must have been well aware that Maginn was a married man with children, and for this reason alone we can dismiss as grossly improbable the account of the affair from the hand of his enemy Berkeley. With long-matured malice he gives in his reminiscences a melodramatic story of his meeting L.E.L. at a party, and being told how she had fallen in love with a writer (whose name she did not at first disclose) and how when she had discovered that he was married she had endeavoured to break off the intimacy; but he had 'persecuted her perseveringly, threatened to expose her, forced from her the greater part of the proceeds of her pen, and, in short, so compromised her that her life had become a burthen to her.' Here he is obviously lying, for though Maginn could be cruel in print his follies in private life were those of weakness and generous irresponsibility and not of meanness, and on this matter one prefers the evidence of famous contemporaries who knew him well to the word of a rake. Berkeley depicts himself as a chivalrous rescuer to whom L.E.L. turned in an affair 'demanding courage, prudence and delicacy, as well as prompt resolution. It was impossible that such an appeal, spoken with all the natural eloquence of sincerity, should be made to me in vain. . . My advice was at once to stop all intimacy with him, to have the door shut in his face if he called; moreover, to refer him to me for an explanation. . . Of course it created the bitterest feelings against us both; the miserable assuming tyrant saw that his prey was at last taken out of his jaws.'[1]

Fears often expressed that L.E.L. was being spoilt by flattery were to be cruelly justified: she paid a heavy penalty for the imprudences of expression that her friends had noted with so much concern. Scandal gathered about her—the names of Jerdan, Maginn and Bulwer Lytton were mentioned as lovers of hers—and this scandal was deliberately fostered by anonymous letters written to her friends in 1830 hinting that she was the mistress of a married man. Her novel *Romance and Reality*, published in 1831, contained glowing portraits of a distinguished writer and his wife, and everyone recognised that Bulwer Lytton and his wife Rosina were the originals. In the following year Maginn selected the novelist as the subject of No. 27 in his Gallery series, and writing with relish about his favourite enemy (then editing the *New Monthly*, a rival magazine) he planted a dart that brought acute embarrassment to both of its victims: 'L.E.L. has so completely depictured *(sic)* him (we shall not say con amore, lest that purely technical phrase should be construed literally). . .' Later L.E.L. was to be the subject of a friendly Gallery article. 'She is a very nice, unbluestockingish, well-dressed, and trim-looking young lady. . .'

Mr. Michael Sadleir, in *Bulwer and His Wife*,[2] devotes an appendix to 'The "Affaire" Bulwer-Landon-Maginn,' in which he stresses that Maginn's acquaintance with L.E.L. began in the 'twenties and suggests that the

---

[1] Not so well known is the fact that Berkeley himself had a long —and respectable—association with journalism. In 1854 he became a regular contributor to the *Field* and wrote for many years on a variety of subjects. 'He was able to paint a country scene in words which showed how deep was his love of the land,' says Mr. R. N. Rose in *The Field: 1853-1953* (Michael Joseph, 1953).

[2] Bulwer Lytton, as we know him, was originally Edward Bulwer.

Bulwers, of whom she had become the intimate friend, used their influence to discourage the attentions of Maginn and that this was the origin of his persistent attacks on the novelist in print. Yet we know that he continued on terms of friendship with L.E.L. for some years afterwards and that as late as 1832 he generously helped her by writing poems that she signed. No one knows who wrote the deadly letters about L.E.L., but it is not believed that it was Maginn's wife. Mr. Sadleir suggests that they were written either by Maginn or at his instigation, and finds support in the fact that the married man whose mistress L.E.L. was alleged to be was not named in the letters. It seems more likely that the anonymous letter-writer was Rosina Bulwer, the spiteful wife, who, writing many years later (1855), alleged that Miss Landon had had liaisons with Bulwer. Maginn and Jerdan and charged her also with the writing of obscene letters—perhaps another example of attack serving as defence, of accusing one's enemy of the crime one has committed oneself. Poor, foolish L.E.L. suffered miserably for her indiscretions of speech. The scandal came to the ears of her fiancé, John Forster—then (1834) only twenty-two and therefore ten years younger than herself—and he broke off their engagement. The later tragedy of her life, her strange marriage and her death from poisoning in West Africa, does not come within the scope of this book.

When the news of her death reached Maginn in 1838 he was deeply affected and 'almost lost his senses for two days.' He was no longer the Maginn who had enjoyed a splendid hour of triumph in the early 'thirties when he was writing his incisive Gallery sketches in 'a Regent Street back parlour.' The shocking affair of the review of Grantley Berkeley's book and its brutal sequel and his disingenuous justification had clouded his reputation. He still wrote brilliantly for the magazines—*Blackwood's*,[1] *Bentley's Miscellany* (he did an amusing prologue for the first number of 1837) and *Fraser's*—and he was contributing to the *Age* and the *Argus* and simultaneously to the Radical *True Sun;* but his constitution had been wrecked by his intemperate habits and he was visibly degenerating. Despite this he did some of his outstanding work about this time—his essays on the learning of Shakespeare, his *Homeric Ballads,* and a mock review of Southey's *The Doctor* that provoked eager, delighted discussion. 'He is a ruin, but a glorious ruin, nevertheless,' wrote the loyal Kenealy. 'He takes no great care of himself. Could he be induced to do so, he would be the first man of the day in literature, or any thing else. But he lives a rollicking life, and will write you one of his ablest articles while standing in his shirt, or sipping brandy— so only do the best and wittiest thoughts flow from his pen.'

It was this spectacle of wasted talent, this shadow of inevitable doom, that haunted the imaginations of his friends, powerless to help him except with money that vanished almost as soon as it was given. They saw in him a man who was supremely gifted—a great scholar and critic, a philosopher 'abler than Coleridge,' a brilliant satirist, an accomplished journalist, a fluent and ingenious parodist and a conversationalist of rare wit and charm— and a man of endearing gentleness and kindliness, 'so different from the fanciful pictures drawn of him by those who had never seen him.'

[1] A few years earlier, in 1834, he had contributed to *Blackwood's* two of his best short stories—'The Story Without a Tail' and 'Bob Burke's Duel with Ensign Brady.' A collection of his stories, under the title *Ten Tales,* was published by the Scholartis Press (Eric Partridge, Ltd.) in 1933—the only work by Maginn to be reprinted in the present century. His *Miscellanies,* in five volumes, were published in New York in 1855-57. They were edited by Dr. R. Shelton Mackenzie, who contributed a long memoir of the writer. No separate biography of Maginn has yet appeared.

There was a brief period during which he edited a provincial weekly, the *Lancashire Herald,* published at Liverpool; but the friendly proprietor was unwise enough to give Maginn the hospitality of a good cellar, and the newspaper failed. About this time, in 1840, he began the publication, in weekly parts, of *Magazine Miscellanies,* selections from his writing, but he had lost his public. Years before there would have been a good sale for the work; now it had to be discontinued after a few numbers. His day was over.

'The Tobias Correspondence,' two satirical letters that appeared in *Blackwood's Magazine* in July and August, 1840, showed no loss of gaiety or confidence, although they were written 'in a little garret in Wych Street, in the Strand, where the Doctor was hiding from the blood-hounds of the law.'[1] The letters purported to be written from Ben Jonson's Head, Shoe Lane, Fleet Street, by Nestor Goosequill, Esq., to Tobias Flimsy, Esq., 'on the general question of editing newspapers.' In No. 1 he wrote:

'You tell me you have taken the office of editor of a newspaper, and seem not a little elated at the dignity—an elation, in esteeming which at its proper value I should have a more ready means of ascertaining, if I had seen your agreement, or knew the present state of the stability of your journal. But you don't tell me what the paper is—where published—how backed—or what politics; and yet, leaving me thus in the dark, you ask me to give you sound practical advice. . .

'But how am I to guide you in the midst of this thick and palpable obscure *(sic)*? Are you Tory, Whig, Radical, Chartist, Low Church, No Church, Snob Church, Rob Church, Up Papist, Down Papist, Voluntary, Involuntary, Intrusionist, Extrusionist, Moderate, Immoderate? Are you in an agricultural district, or in a manufacturing?

[1] *Dublin University Magazine,* January, 1844.

Slavery, or no slavery? Currency solid, or currency paper? What are you? I know not. I have no means of knowing; and yet you ask me to advise how to conduct your paper. I can only return a general answer. . .'

The second letter abounded with advice to the new editor on how to treat various subjects that he would probably be called upon to write about, typical phrases being suggested. 'All the old and venerable battery of rhetoric and argumentation are there ready at hand, piled up like so many bombshells or balls in a besieged battery ready to explode. Two or three have been perhaps damaged by over-use; but it takes a great deal to ruin a well-constructed projectile of force. I mean—1. March of mind. 2. Nineteenth century. 3 Ignorance of past ages. 4. Intelligence of the present—with a few more of these long-known raw materials for leading articles. You cannot do without them; but use them sparingly.' Another suggestion: 'It is hard to make finance what the young ladies call "interesting," but for a good solid plum-pudding article, few things do better.'

Maginn sought a pension from the Tories, but they were aware of his association with Radical journalism and would not help him. His debts eventually brought him into the Fleet Prison, from which he obtained discharge on being declared insolvent. It is to this episode that we probably owe the portrait of him by Thackeray as Captain Shandon in *Pendennis*. The *Dictionary of National Biography* suggests that the true original was John Sheehan, another Irish journalist,[1] but the following extracts from Thackeray's correspondence seem clearly to indicate that the character of Shandon was modelled on Maginn:

From a letter to Mrs. Carmichael-Smythe: 'You will have seen poor Maginn's death in the papers. I thought

[1] *Vide* article on Sheehan.

he could not live a week longer when I saw him in prison before leaving town... He died of sheer drink I fear.'

From a letter to John Douglas Cook (January 8, 1850): 'I have carried money, and from a noble brother man of letters, to some one not unlike Shandon in prison, and have watched the beautiful devotion of his wife in that drear place.'[1] (In *Pendennis* the wife of Captain Shandon is described as a clergyman's daughter—another point of resemblance.)

When Maginn came out of prison he was broken in health and spirit. He was in an advanced stage of consumption and left London to stay at Walton-on-Thames, where he died on August 21, 1842. Sir Robert Peel, who had helped him previously, sent him £100 on hearing of his illness, but this gift did not arrive until the end was near and probably Maginn never heard of this last kindness.

Punch, for which he had started writing with the publication of the Almanac, gave him the first of its black-bordered obituaries: 'We have stepped aside to hang our humble immortelle above the grave of a genius...' Many decades after his death—in 1926—his grandchildren and others interested in his life and work placed a memorial cross over the grave in the churchyard at Walton-on-Thames. It stands on the right-hand side of the main pathway to the church. The epitaph reads:

Sacred to the Memory of
Dr. William Maginn
A Man of Letters
Born in Cork 10th July 1794
Died at Cypress Lodge the 21st August 1842

[1] *The Letters and Private Papers of William Makepeace Thackeray.*

'With Homer and with Shakespeare on the heights
By day he walked; the most "Ambrosian Nights"
Of Maga found him master of the feast;
Then lesser men to fuller fame increased;
Till, Darkly Toiling for his Daily Bread,
Too soon, Alas! he bowed his brilliant head;
Yet, in the very shadow of the Cross,
Found Heaven's great gain, for all earth's little loss.'

A.P.G.

But the epitaph that will be remembered as long as
men read about Maginn is this jestingly affectionate
tribute written by his friend J. G. Lockhart:

'Here, early to bed, lies kind William Maginn,
Who, with genius, wit, learning, Life's trophies to win,
Had neither great Lord, nor rich cit of his kin,
Nor discretion to set himself up as to tin;
So, his portion soon spent (like the poor heir of Lynn),
He turned author, ere yet there was beard on his chin—
And, whoever was out or whoever was in,
For your Tories his fine Irish brains he would spin,
Who received prose and rhyme with a promising grin—
"Go ahead, you queer fish, and more power to your fin!"
But to save from starvation turned never a pin.
Light for long was his heart, though his breeches were
thin,
Else his acting, for certain, was equal to Quinn;
But at last he was beat, and sought help of the bin
(All the same to the Doctor, from claret to gin),
Which led swiftly to jail, with consumption therein;
It was much, when the bones rattled loose in his skin,
He got leave to die here, out of Babylon's din.
Barring drink and the girls, I ne'er heard of a sin—
Many worse, better few, than bright, broken Maginn.

Walton-on-Thames, August, 1842.

Albany Fonblanque
and the 'Examiner'

*

IN the eighteen-thirties there was no wittier or more formidable writer on current affairs than Albany Fonblanque, the journalistic sword of the Radicals, but when he died forty years later he was almost forgotten; and today for one student of nineteenth-century history who knows that he was a distinguished editor of the *Examiner* there are probably a hundred who associate the paper only with the names of the brothers Hunt, who founded it and who suffered imprisonment for an audacious libel on the Prince Regent in its pages. Yet as Leigh Hunt himself said in his autobiography: 'Mr. Fonblanque. . . was the genuine successor, not of me but of the Swifts and Addisons themselves; profuse of wit even beyond them, and superior in political knowledge.'

His fine, impressive name was an inheritance from Huguenot ancestors. His great grandfather, Abel de Grenier, Comte de Fonblanque, decided in 1740 to send his two sons, Antoine and Jean, to England at a time when life was difficult in France for those who professed the Protestant faith. Antoine died without leaving male heirs, and on the death of his father Jean realised as far as possible the family possessions in Languedoc, became a naturalised Englishman and married an Englishwoman: one of their sons, a famous Equity lawyer and a Member of Parliament, was the father of Albany William Fonblanque, who was born in 1793.

In the study of Albany's house in Connaught Square was a framed parchment of a genealogical tree going back five centuries, with an emblazoned coat of arms and a marginal record of the quarterings of successive generations.[1] It is not likely that the friends of the greatest Radical journalist of his time saw anything incongruous in this pride in his aristocratic descent. In the age of transition in which he began to write on politics it was men of wealth and social position who, recognising their social responsibility, were mainly instrumental in bringing about decisive political change. The men who successfully directed the Reform movement were middle-class thinkers such as Jeremy Bentham and James Mill and aristocrats such as Grey, Russell, Durham and Althorp, but for whose resolution in driving through the Reform Bill of 1832 there would have been civil war instead of peaceful revolution. William Cobbett and Francis Place may have been mainly responsible for mobilising public opinion on the side of reform, but it was the initiative of Lord Grey (one of the earliest champions of reform) that broke the resistance of the House of Lords and made the popular will effective.

Fonblanque's father wanted him to make the Army his career and sent him at the age of fourteen to Woolwich to prepare for service in the Royal Engineers, but a severe illness that interrupted his studies for two years led to the abandonment of this plan. Chitty, a famous special pleader of the day, invited him to become his pupil with a view to being called to the Bar. Since Chitty was a friend of his father he did not care to refuse this offer, but he never reconciled himself to the idea of becoming a lawyer, and when he had the good fortune to

---

[1] 'On my once mentioning to my uncle, as an apparent inconsistency, that citizens of the United States frequently exhibited similar documents in their homes, and that, notwithstanding their republican principles, they were prone to point, with aristocratic pride, to a long line of ancestors, he rejoined that he could see no possible connection between a man's political opinions and the interest which it was natural and right for him to take in his family history and antecedents.'—*The Life and Labours of Albany Fonblanque*, by Edmund Barrington de Fonblanque (1874).

achieve some success as a political writer at the age of nineteen he decided that his real career lay in journalism. Excessive application to study of the classics and political philosophy resulted in a second breakdown, and for many years he was handicapped by ill-health. His active journalistic career apparently did not begin until he was about twenty-seven, and during the next ten years he wrote for *The Times,* the *Morning Chronicle,* the *Westminster Review* and other journals, and from 1826 he was principal leader-writer for the *Examiner.*

Within a short time Fonblanque had gained a considerable reputation as a political writer and had become an intimate friend of several of the men who were moulding the political thinking of the new generation—the Mills, Bentham, George Grote and others. In his autobiography John Stuart Mill refers to Fonblanque and John Black (editor of the *Morning Chronicle*) as among the many persons who received and transmitted the influence of his father, James Mill, but says that most of them were accounted as partial allies: 'Fonblanque, for instance, was always divergent from us on many important points.' At all times vigorously independent in his thinking, Fonblanque notably found himself at variance with John Stuart Mill, Grote and their school on the subject of republicanism. He could not share their view of it as the highest of all political conceptions, as the form of government most likely to achieve the Utilitarian ideal of the greatest happiness of the greatest number. What mattered was that the people should be inspired with the spirit of freedom and the love of liberty: whether the head of the state was called a king or a president was comparatively unimportant.

There was nothing facile or accidental about Fonblanque's early success as a political journalist. He had read and thought deeply; he was passionately concerned about the condition of the country and saw clearly what must be done to remove the sense of injustice that poisoned the national atmosphere in the post-Waterloo period; and his ideas were expressed through the medium of a style that was brilliantly effective for its purpose— always clear and virile and persuasive and often penetratingly satirical. He achieved his keen thrust in argument, his admired lucidity in exposition, through the discipline of hard writing: as he told his nephew, in his earlier days he often wrote an article ten times over before it satisfied him and when he saw it in print usually wished that he could rewrite it. When he began to write for newspapers and reviews he was urging reforms that still appeared revolutionary to the majority of the middle and upper classes. The *Edinburgh Review* and other progressive influences had begun to make some impression upon the conscience of the age, but many years would pass before Sydney Smith was able to recall 'a thousand evils. . . which the talents of good and able men have since lessened or removed.' What gave vigour and urgency to Fonblanque's pen was his conviction that unless government was willing to acquiesce in fundamental change the social order, now being increasingly threatened by reckless agitation, would at no distant date have to meet the challenge of widespread violence.

Though they disliked the Press on the whole, governments could no longer gag or intimidate the principal newspapers as they had done in the eighteenth century, and legislation was now mainly directed against the many reckless and irresponsible semi-revolutionary sheets which had been spawned by the mounting discontent. Writing on 'Liberty and Licentiousness of the Press' in the *Examiner* in 1827, apropos of the recent severer enforcement of the law of libel, Fonblanque expressed a strongly Radical view.

'The licentiousness of the Press is a term of the very widest range, including as it does anything that is offensive to anybody. The liberty of the Press, on the other

hand, seems to come under the mathematical definition
of a point—it has neither length, breadth nor thickness.
It is a name representing an impossibility—a publication
useful to the world and offensive to nobody. . . There is
only one body which the Press is permitted to abuse with
entire freedom, and which the more it abuses by false-
hood the more highly its conduct will be extolled by the
authorities. That body, we need hardly say, is the people.
To misrepresent every circumstance of public affairs, to
praise the incapable, call pillage necessary expenditure
and distress prosperity, are falsehoods tending to social
injury which will never be numbered among the offences
of the Press.'

One of his articles—a critique of Moore's *Life of
Sheridan* which he wrote for the *Westminster Review* in
1837—provoked a violent attack on Fonblanque in the
Edinburgh Review. Henry (later Lord) Brougham was
generally thought to be the author, and the sequel
exhibited that strange, brilliant, unlikeable statesman and
lawyer at his most evasive. In reply to a letter from
Fonblanque he wrote:

'I have received your letter of yesterday, in which you
say that you are given to believe that I am the author of
a note in the *Edinburgh Review*, reflecting upon the
publication of private letters in the *Westminster Review*,
and calling upon me to acknowledge it as frankly as you
avow yourself the author of the paper in which these
letters are published.
'I must decline altogether answering any such question,
and I should think that further reflection will convince
you that I can give no other reply to your letter, and that
no inference is to be drawn from it, except my denial of
your right to put the question.'

Fonblanque would not accept this and pressed for an

avowal or disavowal of responsibility. When Brougham
again refused to be drawn he wrote a further letter in
which he tartly commented that the author of the paragraph, whoever he might be, was not a man of honour or
truth. Brougham retorted that it was evidently his wish
to pick a quarrel by fixing upon him a hypothetical
affront. This brought a further letter from Fonblanque,
with this challenge in the ending: 'As to the point of your
feeling yourself insulted by the question whether you
were or were not the author of the paragraph referred
to, I have to say that by the mere inquiry I neither did
nor could mean any offence; but if, notwithstanding this
declaration, you feel yourself aggrieved, I am of course
bound and ready to give you the satisfaction you require.'
The affair now followed the traditional procedure of
those days—up to a point. 'Friends' of the two men took
over and a duel was formally arranged, but at the last
moment Brougham's second raised the objection that
Fonblanque had no right to issue a challenge on such
grounds. It was agreed, after some negotiation, that the
point should be referred for the decision of Lord Dudley,
a friend of both parties, and he gave this ruling: 'Upon
the question, as stated to me, my opinion is, that Mr. F.
is not entitled to call upon Mr. B. to avow whether or
not he is the author of a certain paragraph in the *Edinburgh Review. . .*' A curious affair—and it is difficult to
resist the conclusion that the subtle mind of Brougham
inspired the last-minute suggestion by his second.

Fonblanque's early writing in the *Examiner* brought
into sharp focus many problems affecting the welfare of
the people. Most of his contributions were on political
subjects; but he wrote a number of articles on the admin-
istration of justice and allied topics, including 'The
Magistracy,' 'French and English Libel Law' and 'Game-
Preserving and Man-Destroying.' There was a searching
honesty in Fonblanque's comments on public affairs that
must have disturbed the more conventional-minded

among his readers. He was particularly impatient with
the soft-minded notion (not peculiar to the nineteenth
century) that private virtue is a guarantee of public
worth. While he admired Canning, for instance, he made
the reservation that he was not to be trusted as Prime
Minister simply because he was a good man, and he
made a similar comment about Lord Goderich, who was
in office for a few months. He developed this theme in
lively and satirical fashion in an article written after the
retirement of Goderich in February, 1828.

'Private vices are frequently public virtues. We are
almost tempted to maintain the converse, and to hold
that private virtues are often public mischiefs. George
III's constancy to his wife, and his shoulder of mutton,
his taste for regularity and simplicity, and the blameless
tenor of his domestic life, enabled him to plunge us into
wasting, unjust and unnecessary wars. Had he kept
various concubines, and dined off French dishes at nine
o'clock, the people would have had a lively perception
of the depravity of his politics and an intimate persuasion
of their wrongs. As it was, he soared to heaven between
the shoulders of mutton and the arms of his wife. Two
o'clock dinners and conjugal fidelity procured the remis-
sion of his political sins and his canonisation as a royal
saint. How dearly we have paid for his mutton and his
marital virtue!'

When George IV died in 1830—probably to the relief
of the majority of his subjects—Fonblanque found himself unable to print the usual loyal post-mortem. He left
to others the conventional eulogies and printed a frank
estimate of the late king.

'The historians of the day have not failed to record that
on Saturday the 26th of June the people of this city were
plunged into profound affliction by the decease of George

IV. Shutters before the shop windows denoted the ex-
tremity of national grief. Persons appeared to comport
themselves much as usual, and to the windows of the
shops, not to the windows of the soul, was left the
expression of the deepest sorrow. The bereavement was
mourned by wooden representatives of sadness. Considering the newspaper accounts of the state of popular
sentiment, the manner in which the public commanded
its feelings, and repressed any signs of murmuring at the
decree of Providence, is especially worthy of admiration.

'In his youth he was libertine and profuse, and from
his mature age he showed a preference for persons possessed of no qualities entitling them to consideration or
respect. They have been distinguished by the King's
favour and nothing else—quacks, serviles, sycophants and
buffoons. . . In the personal character of the late King
there is little to praise and much to condemn; and as for
the public events of his reign, for which honour is demanded for him, while in ignorance of his part in the
accomplishment of them, we know not how to concur in
the praise. We must distinguish between the fly on the
chariot and the causes of its course.'

Towards the end of 1830 Fonblanque became editor of
the *Examiner* at the invitation of its owner, Dr. Robert
Fellowes. Announcing this decision to Henry Leigh Hunt,
who had succeeded his father as editor some years before,
Dr. Fellowes wrote: 'I don't suppose there is any more
mystery in the practical part of the management of a
paper than what any man of plain common sense may
master, and Fonblanque will furnish the intellectual in as
much a quantity as the avidity of John Bull for that article
can desire, or his moral stomach digest.' The successful
direction of a serious weekly review, never an easy task
even in the most favourable conditions, was a particularly
exacting one in that age; and within a few years—as will

be seen—Fonblanque, who had by then become owner of the *Examiner*, found himself in difficulties.

The case for freeing the Press from special taxation and bringing journals of repute within the reach of the majority of the people had been vigorously stated by him in an article on 'The Black Art' (1831): 'The disputes about the liberty of the Press will one day be read with as much wonder as the disputes about witchcraft. The belief that helpless old hags could ride the winds, and dispense sickness, sorrow and calamity, will not seem less astonishing than the belief that poor scribblers can exercise baneful powers over the public mind, and order at pleasure the rise and fall of institutions. . . By imposing taxes on newspapers, which place them out of reach of the needy, a contraband trade has been called into existence, and a cheap illicit spirit, ten times above proof, has been hawked among the working classes. The cheap publications, of whose inflammatory tendency so much complaint is made, are the offspring of the stamp duties. Reduce the price of the journals which have some character at stake for truth and knowledge, and this fry would sink in the competition.'

Fonblanque took over the editorship of the *Examiner* a few months before the introduction of the first Reform Bill. Among his contributors was John Stuart Mill, who tells us in his autobiography that the distinguishing character of the paper was given to it entirely by the articles written by Fonblanque, which formed at least three-fourths of all the original matter. 'It is not forgotten with what verve and talent, as well as fine wit, he carried it on, during the whole period of Lord Grey's Ministry, and what importance it assumed as the principal representative, in the newspaper press, of Radical opinions.'

Fonblanque's comments on the 'strangling' by the House of Lords of the first Reform Bill, written on the same day—'the heat of the moment is to be remembered',

as he wrote in a prefatory note in the collected edition
of his articles—were bitter and forthright and hinted that
if Parliament was not reformed the people might be
driven to refusing to pay taxes. That Fonblanque should
have been provoked to writing in this strain is a startling
indication of the dangerous mood of the nation at that
moment. He was no revolutionary and did not even like
to be classed with the 'philosophical Radicals.' He was
essentially a liberal-minded man who saw in the passage
of the Reform Bill the only way to preserve the Constitution.

We have one or two personal glimpses of Fonblanque
about this time. Crabb Robinson in his diary records a
visit to his home in Connaught Square in 1831: '*December
26th.* I found my way to Fonblanque's beyond Tyburn
Turnpike, and dined with him, self-invited. No one but
his wife there, and the visit was perfectly agreeable.
Indeed he is an excellent man. I believe him to be not
a mere grumbler from ill-humour and poverty, as poor
Hazlitt was to a great degree, but really an upright man,
with an honest disgust at inequity, and taking delight in
giving vent to his indignation at wrong. His critical
opinions startle me. He is going to introduce me to
Jeremy Bentham, which will be a great pleasure.' A few
weeks earlier, in a letter to John Sterling (October 22),
John Stuart Mill wrote that Carlyle had, through him,
'sought the acquaintance of Fonblanque (of the *Examiner*), whom I found him to be an admirer of, and who,
though as little of a mystic as most men, reads his
writings with pleasure. I expect great good from Fonblanque; he is fashioned for the work of the day, as
befits one who works for the day, but he is one of those
on whom one may most completely rely for being ready to
turn over a new leaf when the old one is read through.'[1]
Shortly afterwards Carlyle met Fonblanque and took an

[1] *Letters of John Stuart Mill*, edited by Hugh Elliott (Longmans,
1910).

instant liking to this 'long thin man' of 'wrinkly, baggy
face' and keen eyes, and considered him to be the finest
journalist of the day, a man who was in earnest about
improving the conditions of the poor.[1]

The events following the rejection of the Reform Bill
showed that the sombre anticipations of the reformers
had not been exaggerated. The whole country was in a
ferment; there were acts of violence, including rioting at
Bristol and Nottingham; revolutionary orators uttered
wild threats, and reports of drilling by Radicals led many
propertied people to lay in arms. The climax of the
Reform Bill drama came in May, 1832, when William IV
reluctantly accepted Grey's proposal that additional peers
be created to secure the passage of the measure. The
mere threat of this step proved decisive; a sufficient number of peers abstained and the Bill went through.

With reform out of the way Parliament was soon
fiercely engaged once again in a variety of controversies.
Fonblanque continued to pursue his independent line and
fought hard for his favourite causes. The cautious-minded
Crabb Robinson did not like the tone of the *Examiner*
at the beginning of 1833.

'*February 3rd, 1833*. . . .Then I walked to the Athenaeum, where I sat nearly two hours; too much of it lost
napping; but I read the *Examiner* of the day with some
admiration and no pleasure. The bitterness of Fonblanque
becomes every week more offensive, nor is his candour
at all improving. By the bye, in Saturday's *Globe* is a
palpable hit which the *Examiner* will feel:

'To call the stamp duties on newspapers a tax on
knowledge
Is like calling the excise on gin a tax on food.'[2]

[1] *Carlyle to 'The French Revolution,'* by David Alec Wilson
(Kegan Paul, 1924).
[2] From the manuscript of Crabb Robinson's Diary in Dr.
Williams's Library.

Crabb Robinson's gibe was probably little more than the expression of a momentary irritation. His brief experience of editorship of *The Times* a quarter of a century earlier must have given him sufficient insight into the problems of journalism not to underrate the handicap of the newspaper tax, and his previously recorded opinion of Fonblanque made clear that he regarded him as a responsible writer.

Towards the end of 1833 the *Examiner* ran into a crisis from which it was rescued by a remarkable scheme that has no parallel in the history of the British Press. One hundred friends and supporters of the editor paid their subscriptions ten years in advance in order to get the paper out of its difficulties, and the episode gives striking evidence of the unique position of Fonblanque in the journalism of his time. There is a conflict of evidence on the cause of this crisis, but there is no misunderstanding the demonstration of affection, good will and admiration that it evoked.

According to the *Dictionary of National Biography*, which has an excellent memoir of Fonblanque, the money was required 'to defray the cost of improved machinery to allow of its being issued at a lower price. . . and the measure produced a large increase of circulation.' The biography written by his nephew states: 'The high price of the *Examiner* materially limited its circulation among the poorer classes. In order to bring it more within their reach, it was suggested that the cost of the production might be reduced by the use of machinery in printing. . . The arrangement resulted in a large and rapid increase in circulation of the *Examiner*, which was steadily maintained during the next twenty years.'

Bulwer Lytton, a devoted friend of Fonblanque, was one of several influential men who energetically supported the subscriptions-in-advance plan, and among the letters he wrote to friends was one to Disraeli (March 6, 1834). '. . .An opportunity occurs for you to be generous

—and wise. The *Examiner* is in certain straits. A hundred
subscribers are to agree to take it for the next ten years—
paying the subscription in advance now, but on better
terms, i.e., instead of paying £15 or £16, which they
would do in ten years, they are paying £10 now, and for
the next ten years to have the paper *gratis*. The list is
nearly full. About three or four names only are wanted.
Let me advise you to send yours. It will serve a good
paper, a brilliant writer, and on the whole may serve
yourself. *Verb. Sap.* . .'[1] Disraeli's response to Bulwer's
appeal (let us hope not unduly influenced by the rather
cynical ending) was expressed in a characteristic letter
to Fonblanque (March 16, 1834). 'I am sure at the present
day even talent as distinguished as yours must struggle in
vain against machinery—the power which it is well
certainly to have on our side,' he wrote. 'I believe that I
am the last person who ought to bear witness to the
candour or the justice of your strictures; but I am very
willing also to believe that my case is the exception that
proves the rule of your impartiality. I hope therefore you
will permit me to inscribe my name on the list of the
acceders to your proposals.'[2]

We get a different picture of the financial situation of
the *Examiner* in a letter which John Stuart Mill wrote to
Carlyle (December 22, 1833), in which the philosopher
austerely comments on Fonblanque's standard of living.
The paper was not prosperous, but the real cause of its

[1] *The Life of Edward Bulwer, First Lord Lytton*, by his grand-
son, the Earl of Lytton (Macmillan, 1913).

[2] Three years later Thomas Barnes asked Disraeli to review
England under Seven Administrations (a collection of Fonblanque's
articles) for *The Times* and told him: 'Be as severe as you like with
the man, but abstain from all personal attacks on the man in his
private life and conduct.' The review, signed 'From a Correspondent,' ended with this harsh judgment: 'One of the most over-
rated public writers of the day. . . we have thought it worthy of
some trouble to expose the astounding disproportion between his
pretensions and his powers.' (*The History of 'The Times'.*)

difficulties was that Fonblanque had wanted firmness to restrain his expenses within his means. His nominal salary was £500, but this was reduced to £200 by a weekly loss of £6 on the paper. 'He, meantime, has been living at a rate most needlessly expensive, and is at last so completely drained, and his credit I should think so completely exhausted, that he can go on no longer. . . If his difficulties do not ruin the paper it is in no danger, for means of retrenchment present themselves.' Less than the whole hundred advance subscriptions would not do, for the debts amounted to £780, 'and money to the extent of the remainder will then be wanted to start it fair, or perhaps (for I know not) to keep poor Fonblanque out of King's Bench.' The sale of the *Examiner* (Mill added) did not much exceed 3,000 copies.

Mill's cool assessment of the situation gives the true picture. The money was required, as his letters show, to get Fonblanque out of his financial difficulties. There is no evidence that any part of it was used to instal machinery making it possible to lower the price of the paper. The price was sevenpence in 1833, before the subscriptions-in-advance campaign was launched, and as a weekly reminder to the reader about the taxation of the Press the figure was shown as made up of 'Paper, Print, etc. 3d.' and 'Taxes on Knowledge, 4d.';[1] and it continued at this price until the reduction of the stamp duty from fourpence to one penny (September 15, 1836), when it was lowered to fivepence.

Fonblanque was one of several notable writers of the day—Bulwer and Disraeli were others—who were to be seen at the Blessington-d'Orsay parties at Seamore Place and Gore House. When Nathaniel Parker Willis, an American author, published his impression of one of those occasions in a travel letter contributed to the *New*

[1] The 4d. red Government stamp on each copy of the paper included the note '20 per cent. discount.'

York Mirror (later reprinted in his book *Pencillings by the Way*) that ill-naturedly commented on Fonblanque's personal peculiarities, he was sternly rebuked by Bulwer, Lockhart and others. Lady Blessington had an immense admiration for Fonblanque's qualities. 'Lay this man to your heart,' she once wrote to Henry Bulwer, the novelist's brother. 'He is one of those extraordinary men too good for the age in which they are born, too clever not to be feared, instead of loved, and too sensitive and affectionate not to be grieved that it is so.' It was to this most loyal of the many friends of Fonblanque that Willis, strangely insensible of offence, sent a copy of the *New York Mirror* article. It told of his being invited to Lady Blessington's house, and after describing how Henry Bulwer engaged in a discussion on some speech by Daniel O'Connell, went on:

'His opponent in the argument was Fonblanc *(sic)*, the famous editor of the *Examiner*, said to be the best political writer of the day. I never saw a much worse face—sallow, seamed, and hollow, his teeth irregular, his skin livid, his straight black hair uncombed and straggling over his forehead. . .

'A hollow, croaking voice, and a small, fiery black eye, with a smile like a skeleton's, certainly did not improve his physiognomy. He sat upon his chair very awkwardly, and was very ill dressed, but every word he uttered showed him to be a man of claims very superior to exterior attraction. The soft musical voice, and elegant manner of the one, and the satirical sneering tone and angular gesture of the other, were in very strong contrast.'

It was not the accidents of personal appearance that impressed more competent observers. Creevey notes (May 28, 1836); 'Yesterday I dined at Holland House. . . Dr. Lushington and Fonblanque, a son of old Fonblanque,

and writer of one of the cleverest Sunday papers,[1] were
the others [present]. I took to Fonblanque very much.'
The *Greville Diary* has this entry under date March 13,
1836: 'Yesterday I dined with Ben Stanley in Downing
Street, and met Bulwer Lytton and Fonblanque, the latter
a very agreeable man.' Thackeray writes to a friend
(December 20, 1839): 'Fonblanque promised to dine here
t'other day—but refused when he heard of John Kemble's
coming. F. is a very kind and gentlemanlike individual.'[2]
One more reference to Fonblanque from a letter written
by Thackeray to the editor of the *Morning Post* (January
8, 1850), commenting on a leading article dealing with
the status of the literary man in this country: '. . .What
intelligent man, of what political views, would not receive
with respect and welcome that writer of the *Examiner* of
whom your paper once said "He made all England laugh
and think"? Who would deny to that brilliant wit, that
polished satirist, his just tribute of respect and admiration?'

There is a rare unanimity in the favourable judgment
of the contemporaries of Fonblanque (Disraeli is an
obvious exception): even Carlyle, so often tetchy about
his fellow men, was a warm admirer.

Liberal statesmen sought from time to time to recruit
Fonblanque for public service. He refused many such
offers, including the Governorship of Nova Scotia, which
must have had a powerful sentimental appeal for him,
since this proposal was made to him at a time when the
constitutional changes in Canada were moving towards
the self-government of which he had been a constant

---

[1] The *Examiner*, which was dated Sunday but appeared on
Saturday, was described by itself as 'A Sunday Paper on Politics,
Literature, and the Fine Arts.' It was, of course, a weekly review
—not a Sunday paper in the modern sense.
[2] *The Letters and Private Papers of William Makepeace
Thackeray.*

advocate. But eventually, in 1847, domestic reasons led him to accept the post of statistical secretary to the Board of Trade, the offer being accompanied by the express stipulation of Lord John Russell that this public office was not to fetter him in the expression of his political views.[1] He handed over the editorship of the *Examiner* to John Forster but continued to write for the paper until 1860 and retained the proprietorship until 1867. Fonblanque was seen at his most effective in an article on 'The Ballot' that he contributed shortly after he retired from the editorship. 'Open voting is felt to be exposure to intimidation and injury and the security for successful bribery,' he declared. 'It is doomed. The adoption of the ballot is now only a question of time, and the un-English practice of secret voting will be resorted to as the only safeguard against the thoroughly English practice of bullying and bribing.'

It was felt that Fonblanque was becoming more conservative as he grew older, but his writing was as vigorous as ever. He was bitingly satirical, for example, about the official attacks on *The Times* for exposing the scandals of the Crimean campaign.

'The tables are turned. The accusers are accused. The Press is the bane of the Army in the Crimea. "Our own correspondents" have lied away the efficiency of the expedition, and made it falsely believe itself sick, weak, hungry and naked. *The Times* has done it all. As a man may be made ill by telling him he is looking ill, so an Army may be brought to death's door by representations of its jeopardy. . . A slut, rebuked by her mistress for some dirty corner, replied tartly, "La, ma'am, it's not my fault, it's the nasty sun that comes shining into the place and showing every speck." And this is the retort upon

[1] Apparently Fonblanque was again in financial straits, 'arising out of the original purchase of the paper.' See *John Forster and His Friendships,* by Richard Renton (Chapman and Hall, 1912).

the Press, which is charged with the guilt of making the very mischief which it exposes for the purposes of the correction. It is the nasty light, discovering blots and foul places. We wonder that we have not been told that the reason of the superior condition of the French army is not a better organisation and more active care, but simply the absence of a free Press.'

Among those who found no virtue in the later Fonblanque was Sir Charles Gavan Duffy, the Irish politician, and in his *Conversations with Carlyle* he referred to the more recent articles as 'feeble imitations of Fonblanque, wanting in seriousness.' 'Fonblanque is a better man than you suppose—a serious-looking man, with fire in his eyes, Carlyle replied. 'He seems to consider that his task in the world is to expose fallacies of all sorts which in fact he does with considerable adroitness and skill.' Duffy thought that the *Examiner*, once the organ of the educated Radicals, had shifted round and become a Government organ. 'Fonblanque has changed under the influence of circumstances, but not at all with conscious dishonesty,' Carlyle declared. 'Lord Durham when he came home [from Canada in 1838] asked him to dinner and he began to circulate up and down in society yonder in London, and so came to look at government from another point of view. Philosophical radicalism is intrinsically barren. Fonblanque has said all that is in him to say on that.'[1]

A melancholy haze obscures the last years of Albany Fonblanque. Not surprisingly the atmosphere of a government office was uncongenial to him, and only the compulsion of the domestic circumstances alluded to by his biographer could have brought about his relinquishment of the editorship which he had so influentially exercised during many years of important social and political change. His colleagues at the Board of Trade

[1] Quoted in *Carlyle at His Zenith*, by David Alec Wilson (Kegan Paul, 1927).

found him curiously inaccessible but gentle and courteous
to those who came in contact with him. Later this aloof-
ness extended to his social intercourse. He had many
friends of distinction in the worlds of politics and literature—he was a brilliant conversationalist and a sensitive,
amiable man of uncommon social gifts—but his nephew
tells us that during the last ten years he dropped abruptly
out of society. For the last two or three years he retired
completely within himself, and except when he visited
the Athenaeum library or played a game of chess at the
St. James's Club was not seen in public. Although he
lived to be nearly 80 he had suffered from ill-health ever
since his youth. Illness and domestic unhappiness were
thought to be the explanation of his deliberate seclusion
in his last years. In a will dated three months before his
death all his effects (under £3,000) were left to 'my dear
wife Caroline Fonblanque,' with the exception of a
legacy of £100 to his married daughter Rosina. His son,
whose Christian name was also Albany, became known
as a novelist, writing between 1858 and 1892 about a
dozen stories of a melodramatic type as well as more
serious books—*How We Are Governed* and *Rights and
Wrongs* (a manual of household law).

When Fonblanque died on October 13, 1872, few
newspapers published more than a brief mention of the
passing of the man who many years before had made the
Examiner went off like a great gun, echoing all over the
recalled, 'an epigram, a witticism, an illustration, in the
Examiner a great moral force—when, as the *Scotsman*
country.' As the *Examiner* sorrowfully noted: 'The world
has half-forgotten him, or remembers only how a generation or so ago, when his genius was in its prime, he used
to startle his newspaper readers by his brilliant epigrams,
his honest satire and his sparkling wit upon every
political event of importance that occurred.'

The Private Life
of Mr. Bennett

*

ONE of the most stubborn legends of journalism is that the sensational newspaper was the invention of Joseph Pulitzer, who in the eighteen-eighties transformed the *New York World* from a moribund journal into a highly profitable enterprise, and of William Randolph Hearst, who bought the *New York Journal* in 1895 and began a frenzied outbidding of Pulitzer by annexing key men on his staff and turning his new paper (he already owned the *San Francisco Examiner*) into a lurid budget of sex, crime and pseudo-science, with pages of coloured comics. The comic section included a character who was christened the Yellow Kid because he was depicted in that colour, and from this sprang the description of the *World* and the *Journal* as the Yellow Press.

Pulitzer was a man of culture, public-spirited and progressive in his outlook. On assuming control of the *New York World* (May 11, 1883), he promised that his paper would be dedicated to the cause of the people, and a few days later he listed these ten objectives: '1, Tax luxuries; 2, tax inheritances; 3, tax large incomes; 4, tax monopolies; 5, tax the privileged corporations; 6, a tariff for revenue; 7, reform the civil service; 8, punish corrupt office-holders; 9, punish vote-buying; 10, punish employers who coerce their employees in elections.' But there was nothing idealistic in the news columns, the headlines in the early issues of the *World* under his editorship being blatantly sensational.

Hearst was a demagogue in the first stage of his career.

clamorously supporting the popular side on monopolies and similar issues. As a newspaper owner he was cynical, mischievous and irresponsible, and for over half a century (until his death in 1951) the country-wide chain of newspapers that he created was a debasing influence in American life. Of the two men who degraded several New York newspapers into a nightmare of screaming headlines in the 'nineties, Hearst must be assigned the major responsibility: he showed a brutal recklessness that Pulitzer, who was something more than a sensational journalist,[1] would never have attempted to match. It was said of Hearst that he sought to stampede the United States into the war with Spain in 1898 (if he did not actually say, as alleged, to Frederick Remington, 'You provide the pictures, I'll provide the war,' he might well have said it); it was Hearst who conducted a ruthless campaign against President McKinley and published on February 4, 1901 (shortly after the assassination of a Kentucky governor called Goebel), this infamous quatrain written by Ambrose Bierce:

> The Bullet that pierced Goebel's breast
> Can not be found in all the West;
> Good reason, it is speeding here
> To stretch McKinley on his bier.

As if that was not enough the *Evening Journal* two months later said in the course of an editorial: 'If bad

[1] Pulitzer was chosen as the greatest American editor of all time in a poll of daily newspaper editors organised by the *Editor and Publisher* (50th anniversary number, 1934), He was controlling his newspaper from abroad at the time of the battle with Hearst for supremacy—he had almost completely lost his sight through overstrain some years earlier—and when he realised what was happening he put a stop to the worst excesses. In his later years (he died in 1911) the *New York World* mellowed into a responsible newspaper, and when it succumbed to competition in 1931 its passing was regarded as a heavy loss to independent journalism.

institutions and bad men can be got rid of only by killing, then the killing must be done.' Six months later the anarchist Czolgosz shot and fatally wounded McKinley. The storm of anger that swept across the Union when Hearst's incendiary references to the murdered president were recalled had a salutary effect and marked the end of the most vicious phase of Yellow Journalism.

But it was not Joseph Pulitzer, that strange amalgam of brilliant journalist, sensation-monger and idealist, nor William Randolph Hearst, equipped with seven and a half million dollars advanced by his mother to finance his New York invasion—it was neither of these who invented sensational journalism. That discredit belongs to the first James Gordon Bennett, who originated and brazenly exploited the formula half a century earlier.

Nothing could be more unlike the Hearstian debut in New York than the advent of Bennett's daily paper—the *New York Herald* (first called the *Morning Herald*). When he issued the first number on May 6, 1835, his capital was only five hundred dollars, his office was in a cellar and planks laid on two barrels served as a desk (another account says that he used a wooden packing case). It was not his first venture; he had attempted three years earlier to establish a political paper but it lived only a month. A Scotsman by birth, he had come to the United States at the age of twenty-four, and after some teaching experience he worked as a reporter in South Carolina and on New York papers, and eventually became associate editor of the *Courier and Enquirer* in that city. He was forty years old when he started the *Herald*—a man with remarkable powers of work and a man who usually made an unfavourable impression on people. His face was not one to inspire confidence: the mouth was hard and mean, and the eyes had developed a squint through excessive application to printed matter. He liked to suggest that this was not his only point of resemblance to John Wilkes, and he would retort to any comment on his defect that at any rate he was not, as his opponents were, squint-hearted.

In the few years that preceded the first publication of the *Herald* there had been several attempts to widen the appeal of New York journalism. Until then most of the American papers had been blanket-size papers, awkward to handle and ponderous to read, fiercely partisan and limited in sale because they were sold only by subscription, costing ten dollars a year. It occurred to one or two journalists that there must be an opening for cheaper newspapers, wider in their scope and easier to read. Several 'penny'[1] journals were started in American cities, one of the first to gain success being the *Sun* (1833), a four-page quarto-size daily. It was set in small type, the news was given pithily and the stress was on the curious, the sensational and other forms of 'human interest,' the police-court report being the feature with the greatest appeal. Oddly enough New York journals had only recently begun to print police-court news, which had hitherto been austerely excluded as unsuitable for the columns of a newspaper. Their change of policy was prompted by the success in book form of brief chatty reports of the more amusing cases at Bow Street which had appeared in the *Morning Herald* of London, pioneer of a new and lighter technique. These reports do not seem very humorous to a generation that has no liking for the facetious, but they were obviously much to the popular taste in those days.[2] In 1834 another one-cent newspaper—the *Transcript*—was issued in New York,

[1] Then as now a penny signified one cent in American currency.
[2] James Grant, in *The Newspaper Press* (1871), says that the frequenters of public houses and coffee houses, both in town and country, almost demanded that the paper should be bought, and when this was done a notice was posted in the window: 'The *Morning Herald* Taken In.' Within little more than a year the circulation of this sevenpenny journal rose from 1,200 to 3,600. The reports were written by John Wight.

similar in form to the *Sun* but with more emphasis on sensationalism.

It was in this one-cent field that Bennett saw his opportunity. He was temporarily out of work, and his pen had made him many enemies. The *Sun* would not have him on its staff; the earnest, high-minded Horace Greeley, who a few years later founded the *New York Tribune,* was naturally not interested when he suggested that they should go into partnership; so Bennett decided to strike out on his own. He contracted with the printers of the *Sun* to produce his paper, and he issued it in the same handy size. It soon appeared that he had certain professional assets to compensate for the handicap of his meagre capital. He did virtually all the editorial work and the reporting himself, and he was a reporter with a keen news sense and a graphic pen; and he had original ideas, among the earliest being a new type of financial article which he wrote himself and which became indispensable reading in Wall Street. In his reports and his articles alike he revealed a gift amounting to a kind of genius for making his writing vividly intimate and getting the *Herald* talked about. By sheer energy and zest he rapidly developed his paper into a successful rival of the *Sun* and the *Transcript.*

Six months after the start a fire destroyed the printing works and Bennett had to suspend publication for eighteen days. This apparent disaster was the turning-point in the early history of the *Herald.* When the paper reappeared he quickly made good his promise that it would be 'larger, livelier, better, prettier, saucier, and more independent than ever.' No professional inhibitions, no old-fashioned notions about dignity and the right to privacy, were allowed to put any restraint on the selection or the treatment of news. A more responsible editor, Charles A. Dana—whose brilliantly written *New York Sun* became known as 'the newspaperman's newspaper' in the last quarter of the nineteenth century—once uttered the dictum: 'I have always felt that whatever the Divine Providence permitted to occur, I was not too proud to report.' Dana was too intelligent a man to believe this without reservations, but Bennett practised this policy literally and without any check. His paper must be talked about at all costs; he would publish news however shocking it might be (but at the same time sternly rebuke the vicious and establish that he was on the side of virtue), and he would deliberately attack prominent people.

This editorial policy was, of course, attended with certain risks. In New York in the eighteen-thirties, if a man did not like something that a paper said about him he did not write a letter of protest or issue a writ for libel but took up the matter with the editor personally. Bennett had a particular relish for attacking rival journalists, especially his former employer, Colonel James Watson Webb, head of the *Courier and Enquirer*. The day after one attack had appeared Webb met Bennett in Wall Street, knocked him down and thrashed him with a cane. But this was news too. . . Bennett, unashamedly describing the incident in the *Herald*, pictured Webb as coming up behind him and cutting 'a slash in my head about one and a half inches in length, and through an integument of the skull. The fellow, no doubt, wanted to let out the never-failing supply of good humor and wit, which has created such a reputation for the *Herald*, and appropriate the contents to supply the emptiness of his own thick skull. . . He has not injured the skull. My ideas, in a few days, will flow as freshly as ever, and he will find it so to his cost.' On another occasion Bennett was horsewhipped by a Wall Street broker.

The duel in print with Webb continued until one day they came to blows again. Bennett thus reported the clash to his readers:

'As I was leisurely pursuing my business yesterday, in

Wall Street, collecting the information which is daily
disseminated in the *Herald,* James Watson Webb came
up to me, said something I could not hear distinctly, then
pushed me down the stone steps, leading to one of the
broker's offices, and commenced fighting with a species
of brutal and demoniac desperation characteristic of a
fury.

'My damage is a scratch, about three quarters of an
inch in length, on the third finger of the left hand, which
I received from the iron railing I was forced against, and
three buttons torn from my vest, which any tailor will
reinstate for a sixpence. His loss is a rent from top to
bottom of a very beautiful black coat, which cost the
ruffian $40, and a blow in the face, which may have
knocked down his throat some of his infernal teeth for
anything I know. . .

'I tell the honest truth in my paper, and leave the
consequences to God. Could I leave it in better hands?
I may be attacked, I may be assailed, I may be killed,
I may be murdered, but never will I succumb. I never
will abandon the cause of truth, morals, and virtue.'

A few weeks earlier Bennett had set the whole town
talking with his frank reporting of the 'most atrocious
murder' of Ellen Jewett, a good-looking prostitute, and
this scabrous classic of sensational journalism, adroitly
followed up for some days, raised the circulation of the
Herald from 5,000 to 15,000. The girl had been killed
with an axe in a notorious house kept by one Rosina
Townsend, and the murderer set fire to her bed. Bennett
personally visited the scene of the crime: 'like a vampire
returning to a newly found graveyard,' as a critic sourly
commented. He described in great detail the furnishing
of the house and listed the books and magazines in the
murdered girl's room.

'What a sight burst upon me! There stood an elegant

double mahogany bed, all covered with burnt pieces of linen, blankets, pillows, black as cinders. I looked around for the object of my curiosity. On the carpet I saw a piece of linen sheet covering something as if carelessly flung over it.

' "Here," said the police officer, "here is the poor creature." He half uncovered the ghastly corpse. I could scarcely look at it for a second or two. Slowly I began to discover the lineaments of the corpse as one would the beauties of a statue of marble. . .

'The countenance was calm and passionless. Not the slightest appearance of emotion was there. One arm lay over her bosom and the other was averted and hanging over her head. The left side down to the waist, where the fire had touched, was bronzed like an antique statue. For a few moments I was lost in admiration of this extraordinary sight—a beautiful female corpse, that surpassed the finest statue of antiquity. I was recalled to her horrid destiny by seeing the dreadful bloody gashes on her left temple, which must have caused instantaneous dissolution.'

Next day the readers of the *Herald*—some of whom, according to Bennett, had been eagerly pressing shillings into the hands of newspaper boys in Wall Street—were regaled with an outline of the life of Ellen Jewett (her real name was the Puritan-sounding one of Dorcas Doyen). Bennett followed this up with a report of a talk with Rosina Townsend, the first known use of the interview technique in a newspaper. 'For some years she has occupied a brilliant position in the Aspasian society of New York,' wrote Bennett, and one can almost see him pausing to rub his hands before proceeding to embroider this story that was giving such a powerful stimulus to the circulation of the *Herald*. 'Her splendid establishment in Thomas Street has been the pride of the gay young reprobates from one end of the Union to the other.'

'Behind the pile of elegant buildings was a garden decorated with elegant arbors, picturesque retreats, covered in the summer season with beautiful garlands, evergreens, flowers, and all the beauties of the vegetable world. Under the bright shining moon, climbing up the dark blue heaven, during soft summer months these arbors would be filled with syrens and champagne, pine apples, and pretty *filles de joie,* talking, chattering, singing, and throwing out all the blandishments their talents could muster.'

When a young clerk was put on trial for the murder (he was acquitted) the moralist Bennett wrote this smug comment: 'The evidence in this trial and the remarkable disclosure of the manners and morals of New York is one of those events that must make philosophy pause, religion stand aghast, morals weep in the dust, and female virtue droop her head in sorrow.' Never again did Bennett have a news story that gave such rich scope to his peculiar talents; for the most part he had to be content with dabbling in petty obscenities, violating the privacy of his fellow-citizens and throwing mud at his opponents. He doubled the price of the *Herald* but the circulation kept on mounting: he boasted to his readers of the success with which he had introduced novelty into the daily press. 'I have infused life, glowing eloquence, philosophy, taste, sentiment, wit and humor into the daily newspaper. . . Shakespeare is the great genius of the drama—Scott of the novel—Milton and Byron of the poem—and I mean to be the genius of the daily newspaper press.' Not for Bennett the old-fashioned tradition that made the editor an aloof, dignified figure: he delighted in boasting and in breaking down the barriers of good taste, for he knew that his unconventionality would shock people into talking about him and his paper.

'We do not, as the Wall Street lazy editors do, come

down to our office about ten or twelve o'clock, pull out
a Spanish cigar, take up a pair of scissors, puff and cut,
cut and puff for a couple of hours, and then adjourn to
Delmonico's to eat, drink, gormandize, and blow up our
contemporaries. We rise in the morning at five o'clock,
write our leading editorials, squibs, sketches, etc., before
breakfast. From nine till one we read all our papers and
original communications, the latter being more numerous
than those of any other office in New York. From these
we pick out facts, thoughts, hints and incidents, sufficient
to make up a column of original, spicy articles. . .'

But even the readers of the *Herald* must have been
taken aback when they opened the paper for June 1, 1840,
and read this announcement of his impending marriage:

TO READERS OF THE HERALD
Declaration of Love—Caught at Last—Going to be
Married—New Movement in Civilization
'I am going to be married in a few days. The weather
is so beautiful—times are so good—the prospects of
political and moral reform so auspicious, that I cannot
resist the divine instinct of honest nature any longer—so
I am going to be married to one of the most splendid
women in intellect, in heart, in soul, in property, in
person, in manners, that I have yet seen in the course of
my interesting pilgrimage through life. . .
'I cannot stop in my career. I must fulfil that awful
destiny which the Almighty Father has written against
my name in broad letters of light against the wall of
Heaven. I must give the world a pattern of happy wed-
ded life, with all the charities that spring from a nuptial
love. In a few days I shall be married according to the
holy rites of the most holy Christian church to one of the
most remarkable, accomplished, and beautiful young
women of the age. She possesses a fortune—a large
fortune. She has no Stonington shares or Manhattan

stock, but in purity and uprightness she is worth half a million of pure coin. Can any swindling bank show as much? In good sense and elegance another half a million; in soul, mind and beauty, millions on millions. . .

'Association, night and day, in sickness and in health, in war and in peace, with a woman of this highest order of excellence, must produce some curious results in my heart and feelings, and these results the future will develop in due time in the columns of the *Herald*.'

It was in the same year that what became known as the 'Moral War' was declared on Bennett. Several New York contemporaries, whose lead was followed by newspapers in other American cities, urged respectable people to boycott the *Herald*. The epithets that Colonel Watson Webb used in the *Courier and Enquirer* were typical of the Press comment at this time: Reckless depravity; unprincipled adventurer; disgusting obscenity; revolting blasphemy; moral leprosy; ribald vehicle; vile sheet. Committees of leading citizens were organised to support the movement, and they used their influence to get advertisers to withhold their announcements. For some months Bennett was under continuous attack; he was now being talked about in a way that was greatly to his disadvantage; and he felt the effects of this campaign for several years and was under a moral stigma for the rest of his life. From 1840 to 1845 the circulation of the *Herald* dropped from 17,000 to 12,000. Bennett had to give heed to public opinion and to make an effort to improve the tone of his paper.

About this time Horace Greeley, who it will be recalled had refused to go into partnership with Bennett, started a daily of his own that soon became a major political influence. First published on April 10, 1841, the *Tribune* promised to 'advance the interests of the people, and to promote their Moral, Political and Social well-being. The immoral and degrading Police Reports, Advertisements,

and other matter which have been allowed to disgrace
the columns of one leading Penny Paper, will be carefully
excluded from this, and no exertion spared to render it
worthy of the virtuous and refined, and a welcome
visitant at the family fireside.' Some of the 'advanced'
political ideas that found expression in the columns of
the *Tribune*—Greeley was a supporter of Fourierism
among other causes—startled conventional New Yorkers,
but however wrongheaded on certain subjects the paper
might appear to readers there could be no doubt that it
was honestly conducted. Within a short time it had built
up a good circulation for those days. Figures for 1842
credited it with 9,500 as against 15,000 for the *Herald*.
Greeley became a great moral force and the most powerful journalist in the country.

The *Herald* did not recover from its setback until the
Mexican War of 1846-48, which gave scope for enterprise in reporting (almost incredibly, it was the only
New York paper with its own war correspondent) and
raised the circulation to 30,000. During the Civil War,
when the paper had as many as sixty correspondents in
the field, the circulation passed the 100,000 mark. Bennett
owed much of his success to his consistent enterprise, and
he spent money freely to get the news ahead of his rivals.

James Gordon Bennett died on June 1, 1872, at the age
of 76. The next day's issue of the *Herald*, a sixteen-page
Sunday edition sold at five cents, limited its notice of the
event to a leading article about a column in length.

'It is not our province to eulogize the deceased. His
career as a journalist is before the world and is public
property. It will be commented upon, wherever civilization reaches, by friends and enemies; for no man could
hold in his hands so formidable a power as an independent, fearless press and hope to escape the latter. His
death will be mourned by all who regret the passing
away of the sterling benefactors of the human race; for

no one will gainsay the benefits conferred upon mankind by the genius, energy and liberality of the deceased. To him more than to any other individual the American newspaper owes its present high and honourable position. . .'

Newspapermen familiar with the early history of the *Herald,* and with Bennett's delight in those days in exuberant self-revelation in print, noted thoughtfully this dignified reservation in the leading article: 'The private life and personal character of the deceased are the property of his family and friends.' What his wife thought of the publicity given to their marriage has escaped record, but it is known that the 'Moral War' brought her many social embarrassments and that when her two surviving children reached school age she took them to Europe to have them educated there and rarely visited America.

No biography was printed in the *Herald.* In the next day's issue a whole page was devoted to extracts from New York newspapers' articles on Bennett, and extracts from the journals of other American cities continued to appear for some days. The *Herald* did not even print its own report of the funeral, which took place on June 13, but gave extracts from other newspapers under the heading: 'Accounts of the Leading Morning and Evening Papers.' These accounts included rich specimens of morticians' prose that would have satisfied Bennett with his insistence on specific description. The *New York Sun* stated: 'The casket in which the remains of Mr. Bennett are enclosed is remarkable for its elegance. It is nearly square, and made of a species of wood said to be more durable than any metal. . . The entire casket is surrounded by a massive moulding of silver, forming a framework that will survive the lapse of ages.' The *New York Times* noted: 'The features of the deceased were natural and lifelike, although the process of embalming gave the face a ruddier tint than Mr. Bennett possessed.' The leading newspaper editors of New York acted as pall-bearers.

The task of 'eulogizing' which the *Herald* had disclaimed was firmly undertaken by the Boulevard Club (described as 'The neighbours of Mr. Bennett'), who passed a resolution of sympathy, published in the issue for June 5, that began with these words: 'Whereas the Creator and Sovereign of the Universe has removed, by death, from this earthly sphere, after long years of labour, enterprise and perseverance in the beneficial endeavor to elevate and enlighten the human race, James Gordon Bennett, whom no country can claim exclusively, who, by means of his noble characteristics and the wisely directed powers of his pen and press, has spread abroad information and instruction throughout the civilized world and even in those remote regions of Asia and Africa which are but newly penetrated and explored. . .'

The epitaph written by the *New York Tribune* was simpler: 'He developed the capacities of journalism in a most wonderful manner, but he did so by degrading its character. He made the newspaper powerful, but he made it odious.'

POSTSCRIPT.—James Gordon Bennett, junior, succeeded to the ownership of the *Herald* and controlled it for nearly half a century: he was about the same age as his father when he died in 1918. His direction of the paper, mainly exercised from abroad, was marked by considerable enterprise (as, for instance, when—in conjunction with the *Daily Telegraph*—he sent H. M. Stanley to find Dr. Livingstone) and by violent eccentricities in his relations with his staff. He started a Paris edition of the paper in 1887. After his death the *Herald* was bought by Frank A. Munsey, who in 1924 sold it for five million dollars to the Ogden Reid family, who owned the *New York Tribune*. The two papers were

merged as the *New York Herald Tribune.* The story that
began with the calculated pandering of James Gordon
Bennett's *New York Herald* in 1835 and the sincere but
muddled idealism of Horace Greeley's *New York Tribune*
in 1841 has a fortunate sequel: the *New York Herald
Tribune* is a leader of American journalism, a first-class
newspaper with an international reputation for sobriety
and balance.

In the United States as in this country the excesses of
sensational journalism have at all times supplied a ready
weapon to critics of the Press and led to sweeping con-
demnation that has obscured the achievement of the
numerous serious newspapers. Among the contemporaries
of the first Bennett were able editors who maintained the
highest standards of journalism. Greeley has already been
mentioned; another was Samuel Bowles, who in 1844
turned the weekly *Springfield Republican* into a daily
and by sheer force of character made this newspaper
published from a small Massachusetts town (its popula-
tion at mid-century was under 12,000) a vital influence
in national life. In the present century we have seen
distinguished examples of the triumph of responsible
journalism in the United States—notably that of the
New York Times. When Adolph S. Ochs, a 37-year-old
newspaper publisher from Chattanooga, gained control
of the paper in 1896 it was printing only 19,000 copies,
half of which were being returned unsold. His answer to
Yellow Journalism was to produce a newspaper with the
avowed policy, then as now, of giving its readers 'All the
News that's Fit to Print.' He promised that it would 'give
the news impartially, without fear or favour,' and
advertisements proclaimed 'It does not soil the breakfast
cloth.' The subsequent development of the *New York
Times* under the enlightened direction of Ochs and his
successors—its sale is now about 600,000—is too familiar
to need retelling here.

When the reproach is made that the twentieth century

has seen revivals of sensational journalism that can match Bennett, Hearst and Pulitzer at their worst, it may fairly be pointed out that during the same period newspapers of the highest standards have achieved massive gains in circulation and attained a total readership far in excess of what seemed probable even to the most optimistic fifty years ago, and that the sensational journal is the exception and not the rule.

Bibliography. Works consulted in the writing of this chapter include: *American Journalism,* Frank Luther Mott (Macmillan, 1947); *Journalism in the United States,* Robert W. Jones (E. P. Dutton, 1947); *The James Gordon Bennetts,* Don C. Seitz (Bobbs-Merrill, 1928); the *New York Herald* file at the Newspaper Library.

INDEX

GEORGE ALLEN & UNWIN LTD
London: 40 Museum Street, W.C.1

Auckland: Haddon Hall, City Road
Sydney, N.S.W.: Bradbury House, 55 York Street
Cape Town: 58–60 Long Street
Bombay: 15 Graham Road, Ballard Estate, Bombay 1
Calcutta: 17 Chittaranjan Avenue, Calcutta 13
New Delhi: 13–14 Ajmere Gate Extension, New Delhi 1
Karachi: Haroon Chambers, South Napier Road, Karachi 2
Toronto: 91 Wellington Street West
Sao Paulo: Avenida 9 de Julho 11388–Ap. 51

THE MARCH OF JOURNALISM

by Harold Herd

"A highly competent piece of work, a good conspectus of the crowded field, periodicals as well as newspapers. No recent book has quite the same scope and Mr. Herd's work can be especially commended to all young newspapermen."

MANCHESTER GUARDIAN

"It is a work of very readably presented scholarship."

TRUTH

"There was a need for such a book and Mr. Herd has well supplied it."

THE SPECTATOR

Demy 8vo   21s. net

IN PRAISE OF NEWSPAPERS
AND OTHER ESSAYS

by Karel Capek

"His capacity for surprise at what most of us take for granted is refreshing and salutary and gives him in his work a charmingly individual standpoint."

PUNCH

Crown 8vo   8s. 6d. net

*

GEORGE ALLEN & UNWIN LTD